ON THE DIRTY PLATE TRAIL

Harry Ransom Humanities Research Center Imprint Series

PUBLISHED FROM THE COLLECTIONS OF THE HRC

Stuart Gilbert, *Reflections on James Joyce: Stuart Gilbert's Paris Journal*, ed. Thomas F. Staley and Randolph Lewis. 1993

Ezra Pound, *The Letters of Ezra Pound to Alice Corbin Henderson*, ed. Ira B. Nadel. 1993

Nikolay Punin, *Nikolay Punin: Diaries, 1904–1953*, ed. Sidney Monas and Jennifer Greene Krupala, trans. Jennifer Greene Krupala. 1999

Aldous Huxley, *Now More Than Ever*, ed. David Bradshaw and James Sexton. 2000

Stanley Burnshaw, *The Collected Poems and Selected Prose*. 2000

Laura Wilson, *Avedon at Work: In the American West*. 2003

Kurt Heinzelman, ed., *The Covarrubias Circle: Nickolas Muray's Collection of Twentieth-Century Mexican Art*. 2004

Megan Barnard, ed., *Collecting the Imagination: The First Fifty Years of the Ransom Center*. 2007

William Goyen, *Goyen: Autobiographical Essays, Notebooks, Evocations, Interviews*, ed. Reginald Gibbons. 2007

*Edited with
Introduction and
Commentaries by
Douglas Wixson*

On the Dirty Plate Trail

REMEMBERING THE DUST BOWL REFUGEE CAMPS

Texts by SANORA BABB
Photographs by DOROTHY BABB

University of Texas Press *Austin*

All photographs are courtesy of the Harry Ransom Humanities Research Center, The University of Texas at Austin.

Excerpt from *Whose Names Are Unknown* © 2004 University of Oklahoma Press. Reprinted with permission.

Printed in the United States of America
First edition, 2007

Requests for permission to reproduce material from this book should be sent to:
Permissions
University of Texas Press
P.O. Box 7819
Austin, TX 78713-7819
www.utexas.edu/utpress/about/bpermission.html

LIBRARY OF CONGRESS CATALOGING-IN-PUBLICATION DATA

Babb, Sanora.

On the dirty plate trail : remembering the Dust Bowl refugee camps / texts by Sanora Babb ; photographs by Dorothy Babb ; edited with introduction and commentaries by Douglas Wixson. — 1st ed.

p. cm. — (Harry Ransom Humanities Research Center imprint series)

Includes bibliographical references and index.

ISBN-13: 978-0-292-71445-8 ((cl.) : alk. paper)

ISBN-10: 0-292-71445-9

1. Migrant labor—United States—History—20th century. 2. Migrant agricultural laborers—United States—History—20th century. 3. Labor camps—United States—History—20th century. 4. Dust Bowl Era, 1931–1939. 5. Dust storms—Great Plains—History—20th century. I. Babb, Dorothy, 1909– II. Wixson, Douglas C. III. Title.

HD5856.U5B33 2007

331.5'440979409043—dc22 2006028924

ISBN 978-0-292-72144-9 (paperback)

For Suzanne

No writer will write well of people to whom he does not belong; *he belongs only when his roots are so deep down that like the oak he cannot be transplanted—at least in imagination.*

J. FRANK DOBIE

CONTENTS

(Sanora Babb's texts are in italics)

LIST OF ILLUSTRATIONS

MIGRANT FARMER

Self-pity is not their way of telling you:
This migrant life is hard.
That it is unaccustomed and deplored.
The wives say almost half apologetically:
"You must excuse the way things look;
We ain't yet used to managing this way,
But we'll soon learn."

But there's fine dignity the way
They manage in too-small tents with beds
Along each wall—a tin camp stove
Not more than two feet high, and dirt floors
That run with water when it rains.

One family said: "The rats are awful bad.
They come in off the fields." And smiled:
"They must be hungry too." Four pork chops
Sizzled on the tin camp stove—their first
Meat in three months. They asked us
If we wouldn't share their meal. They said:
"There's plenty. Don't go now." It was
Their ever-flowering sense of hospitality,
Not dead, but just the same as if we'd been
A caller come to visit them at home.

Some people seem to think they had no homes;
That migrant farmers never owned a farm,
But came out West from downright laziness
To leech upon the bounty of the rich,
The corporation-farms and state relief.

To see a strong man flat upon his back,
Too weak to move because there was no food,
No work, and no relief. To hear him say:
"We'll find a way out yet. We ain't give up,
But we won't go on starving." *To see a woman*
With a wordless grief because she knows her baby
Must be born on old newspapers in a leaky tent,
(The county hospital has refused her aid),
To see these people shyly seek relief,
Knowing that only hunger brought them there,
Because their pride and courage always frowned
Upon receiving money without work,
Is like a knife-thrust to complacency,
Or attitudes of "Oh, they'll get along."
They'll get along.

Farmers, with no farms to farm,
With intermittent work at pittance pay,
Relief *checks much too small or none at all,*
There is a beauty in the earnest way
You say "We'll get along."
And there is strength behind these simple words,
A challenge, like a promise to be kept.

DOROTHY BABB,
IN *Direction* 7 (SUMMER 1944): 15.

PREFACE

As I complete the final draft of this book, refugees from Hurricane Katrina flee flood-stricken New Orleans and other devastated Gulf cities. Little in the initial response of the federal and state governments to the present calamity shows evidence of having learned from the experience of the Dust Bowl refugees or modeled their relief measures on the Resettlement Administration and its successor, the Farm Security Administration, of seventy years ago.[1]

Longer than recorded history, mass displacements of people, uprooted by famine, war, disease, natural disaster, or economic failure, have created permanent migration flows that move through and around human settlement. In the long chronicle of uprooting and dispossession a single episode resembles every other in its account of losses and gains; only the proportion of each differs. Forced by extenuating circumstances or drawn by the promise of a better life, people will take great personal risks, severing ties with place, loosening personal bonds, forgoing familiar resources. They become migrants: marketable human commodities, statusless outsiders, figures in statistical surveys. The terms of their contingent status frequently compel migrants to accept undesirable living and work conditions, discrimination, and exclusion. As individuals they are condemned to silence, valued for their labor power, not for other human attributes they possess. Driving through California's agricultural valleys travelers glimpse brown-skinned migrants harvesting in fields, timeless figures of toil like Millet's "Gleaners." In the cities Spanish-speaking workers lay masonry foundations and blow leaves from suburban lawns. Across the land a perpetual flow of migrants moves like shifting currents of water, forming transitory subcultures of work—separate, little noticed, yet indispensable to our economy.

For generations, non-native-born workers—Mexican, Filipino, Asian—have planted, pruned, and harvested California's farmlands and orchards. For a relatively brief time, however, from about 1935 to the early years of World War II, dispossessed Anglo-Americans, mainly from the Great Plains, accomplished the main field labor in California's fertile valleys. "Okies" is a term familiar to every high school student assigned to read Steinbeck's *Grapes of Wrath.* The notoriety accompanying the publication of photographs of the Anglo refugees made by a handful of Farm Security Administration (FSA) photographers, as well as the publication of Steinbeck's novel (1939), erupted into cries for reform in response to what was then viewed as a national scandal. The silence that for generations had enclosed immigrant workers was suddenly shattered. It was considered intolerable, as Walter J. Stein notes in *California and the Dust Bowl Migration,* that Anglos should experience conditions viewed as normal for immigrants and blacks.

If the short episode of the migrant Okies attracted the nation's attention only briefly, university researchers, historians, and labor activists have long addressed the problems and prospects of labor migration. Within the ranks of the migrants themselves labor leaders emerged who, like César Chávez, were not content to let consumers purchase their vegetables without wondering under what conditions they were produced.

Earlier bracero (guest worker) programs have yielded today to an accelerating and nearly uncontrolled flow of Latino workers consisting for the most part of undocumented Mexican migrants arriving through the southwestern border states. Recent trends indicate the permanent settlement of families, the result of the unremitting demand for cheap, skilled labor, lax migration controls, established migrant networks, and sporadic legislation legalizing migrants. Every year since 1995 nearly half a million Mexicans have entered the United States to find work, according to Fernando Lozano Ascencio.[2] By January 2004, 5.3 million undocumented immigrants, 57 percent of a total of 9.3 million, had arrived in the United States from Mexico. Some 9 percent of the population born in Mexico live today in the United States. And those numbers continue to increase.

The largest share of immigrant workers from across the southern border are located in California and Texas, yet increasingly the migrant flow of workers has shifted to other parts of the country where work can be found in poultry processing, construction, and agriculture.[3] The sheer push-pull dynamics of migration have made immigrant workers, of whom the majority today are illegal, permanent constituents of American culture and the economy. Apart from providing a cheap pool of ready labor, they contribute tax revenues. In Chicago, for instance, of approximately 300,000 illegal immigrants 70 percent pay into Social Security and unemployment insurance, according to a study by the

Center for Urban Economic Development at the University of Illinois at Chicago.[4]

A small number of writers from within the ranks of the migrants have given voice to the voiceless workers, putting a human face on sociological statistics and inscribing individual lives in the broad sweep of labor history.[5] Sanora Babb (1907–) was not a migrant worker, but she wrote from within the experiences and everyday life of the dispossessed Anglos who were pulled into the migrant flow by economic failure and natural disaster. Born in Oklahoma, raised on the High Plains, an experienced journalist and labor activist, Babb was well situated and well equipped to make good journalistic and literary use of her position tending the "Okies" as assistant to FSA camp administrator Tom Collins. The field notes and journal she kept during her stay in the fields (1938–1939) have never been published. Nor have the photographs of the migrant workers—Anglo, Mexican, and black—with whom she lived in the FSA camps. By grounding a brief but significant chapter of the long history of internal migration in personal narrative and personal observation, these texts and photographs together give an incomparable testimony to an important and tragic episode in American life.[6]

This book is part of a project of literary recovery that began some ten years ago with the intent of drawing readers to Sanora Babb's remarkable legacy of work while laying the groundwork for its interpretation. The span of the entire project, of which the present book is one of several outcomes, includes numerous visits with Sanora Babb; interviews of former Dust Bowl refugee-farmers and their now-grown children and of informants in the three-state area (Oklahoma, Colorado, Kansas) where the Babb sisters grew up; extensive reading of source material; the reprinting of two of Babb's novels and the first-time publication of a third, her Dust Bowl novel *Whose Names Are Unknown*; the creation of an archive at the Harry Ransom Humanities Research Center containing Sanora's papers and Dorothy's photographs; and ultimately a full-length study of the Babb sisters' lives and creative work. Sanora and Dorothy, like the Brontë sisters, shaped their own worlds from materials that less imaginative minds might have failed to notice.

Researchers who study literary production and reception have argued convincingly that the institutions that control publication and set standards of judgment act to mainstream certain works while ignoring others that are deemed of regional interest or that speak to the concerns of working-class people. Such arguments are seldom heard today, drowned out by the sheer volume of popular fiction produced, causing booksellers to move works of literary quality to the back of the store to join other prestigious but little-read works. The difficulty of obtaining a hearing for serious work that lies beyond the bounds of acceptability (and marketability) established by current publishing and merchandising standards makes crucial the task of recovery. This task includes establishing a work's significance within an appropriate framework of values, aesthetic, historical, and sociological. As Alan Wald, Cary Nelson, and others have pointed out, one justification for recovering a long-forgotten text, or situating a recent but ignored one, has to do with the need for diversity of literary expression in the face of institutionalizing forces, whether in academia, in the media, or among general readers who depend on the opinion of others to make their choices.

A gift of a Kodak camera when she was a child initiated Dorothy's lifelong love of photography. The legendary cinematographer James Wong Howe, the Babb sisters' close friend, gave Dorothy and Sanora Leica and Rolleicord cameras when he learned of Sanora's intent to work with the Farm Security Administration in 1938 setting up tent camps for the farmer-refugees. The sisters had worked as informal collaborators since their early days on the High Plains, where, seeking relief from penury and isolation, they read to one another, performed dramas, and published their poems in magazines. Sanora, strong-willed and vibrant, inevitably took the lead; Dorothy, richly talented but diffident, kept to herself. A 1935 graduate of English literature at UCLA, Dorothy offered her sister revisions and suggested topics. Yet Dorothy was reluctant to let the world see her own work. Dorothy shrank before the world; Sanora embraced it with whole heart. Dorothy's photographs were gathering dust when Sanora drew my attention to them several years ago. "You might find these photographs interesting," she said.

ACKNOWLEDGMENTS

In recovering these texts and photographs and revealing their significance, I gratefully acknowledge the assistance of many good people who have lent support, provided information, shared memories and materials, and given encouragement. Foremost, of course, is Sanora Babb, whose cheerful patience and vivacious spirit graced my many visits.

Of Sanora's many friends, I am particularly indebted to her nephew Don Lee, librarian at the Academy of Motion Picture Arts and Sciences in Beverly Hills, California, and her literary agent, Joanne Dearcopp. Others close to Sanora have kindly shared their reflections and memories, among them Roxana Ma Newman, John Michaan, Leigh Taylor-Young, Bonnie Barrett Wolfe, Ray Bradbury, and Asa and Alba Zatz. By letter or directly I was able to interview writers, literary agents, film production people, and political activists who knew Sanora well, including Richard Bach, Julie Fallowfield, Bernard Gordon, Sylvia Jarrico, Peter Keane, C. Y. Lee, Peg Nixon (Margaret McCord), Tillie Olsen, John Sanford, Roslyn Sharp, Wilma Shore Solomon, Lawrence Spingarn, Sid Stebel, Janet Stevenson, Haskell Wexlar, and Harriet Woods. In addition, I owe much to fellow researchers David Anderson, Jackson Benson, Roger Bresnahan, John Crawford, Gerald Haslam, Philip Herring, Bob Hethmon, Julia Mickenberg, Cary Nelson, Larry Rodgers, Alex Saxton, Jerry Shepperd, Stephen Wade, Alan Wald, David Weiner, and Fred Whitehead. Seema Weatherwax, whose photographs are a remarkable record of migrant life, generously recalled her visits to the FSA camps. Dorothy Ray Healey remembered Sanora from a farm strike in which they both took part. Tillie Olsen and Meridel Le Sueur, fellow radical activists and writers in the 1930s, shared their reminiscences. Surviving members of the King family—Julia, Charlie, Harlan, and Bill—recalled in detail their odyssey west from Arkansas to California, their days in the fields and nights entertaining the migrant labor camp people with "Soldier's Joy" and "Sally Goodin." David Douglas Duncan drew my attention to the photographer Horace Bristol, who worked with Steinbeck. Ever discerning and insightful, Suzanne Chamier Wixson was my mainstay throughout the project.

I was fortunate to have been able to interview several of Sanora's childhood friends, including Irene Hutchens Harrington, Fay Harrington Day, and Mollie Lee (Bowles) Beresford. Already in their nineties when I interviewed them, Nelson Parks and Mildred Parks Patterson, the Babb sisters' first cousins, recalled with vivid detail their early years together as children. Their affection for Sanora and Dorothy extends to both Nelson's and Mildred's children, Aleta, Dell, Patsy, Colette, Cheryl, Jerry, and Jim, who came to Waynoka, Oklahoma, in October 2004 for my lectures on Sanora's work. The recognition that gradually brings critical attention to a writer's work frequently begins with a small number of dedicated readers and grows as their devotion ripples out to others.

In the matter of source materials I depended greatly on the generosity of local historians: Olga Montgomery (Finney County Historical Society, Garden City, Kansas); Katherine Hart (Finnup Foundation); Dr. Pauline Morgan (Forgan, Oklahoma); Iris Lochner (Edmond, Oklahoma); Sandie Olsen and Carol King (Waynoka Historical Society, Waynoka, Oklahoma); Elmer D. Moore (McLouth, Kansas); Lynn Housouer (Imperial County Historical Society, El Centro, California); Stacy Vellas (Pioneer Museum, El Centro, California); Doris Weddell (Bakersfield, California); Helen C. Brown (Morton County Historical Society, Kansas); Erma Hall Williams (Springfield, Colorado); Joy Lepel (Baca County Museum, Springfield, Colorado); Ike Osteen (Springfield, Colorado); Kathleen and Jack Dawson (Two Buttes, Colorado); Virginia Campbell (Two Buttes, Colorado); Constance Harper (Red Rock, Oklahoma); Ted Cass (Sullivan, Maine); John Frazier (Garden City, Kansas); Imogene Beaumont (Gig Harbor, Washington); Wilma Elizabeth McDaniel (Tulare, California); Mary Turner (Edmonds, Washington); Kenneth R. Turner (No Man's Land Historical Society); Fanny Judy (Jones-Plummer Trail Museum, Beaver, Oklahoma); Dwight Leonard (Beaver, Oklahoma); Tudi Arneill and Fran Blanchard (Plains Conservation Center, Aurora, Colorado). The University of Oklahoma Press graciously permitted me to use a section from Babb's *Whose Names Are Unknown.*

In addition, I wish to thank the archivists at the Oklahoma Historical Society; the Tulsa Public Library; the Los Angeles Public Library; the Manuscript Department, Prints and Photographs Division, Library of Congress; the Federal Records Center, San Bruno, California; the Bancroft Library, University of California, Berkeley; Special Collections, Stanford University; and the Wichita State University Libraries. I also wish to thank Barbara Hall and Don Lee, Margaret Herrick Library, Academy of Motion Picture Arts and Sciences; Jeannie Girard, Jeff Rankin, and Dale Trevelyean, UCLA Oral History Archive; Dale Heckendorn, Colorado Historical Society; Sarah Cooper and Mary Tyler, Southern California Library for Social Studies and Research; Irene Still Meyer, California State University–Long Beach; Carol Fonken and Joan Parks, A. Frank Smith, Jr. Library, Southwestern University; and Mike Childers, video specialist.

The Harry Ransom Humanities Research Center, University of Texas, Austin, is an extraordinary resource with an expert staff, unfailingly cheerful and generous; a large thank-you to Liz Murray, Cathy Henderson, Jean Townsend, Pat Fox, Bob Taylor, Richard Workman, Travis Willmann, Elizabeth Garver, and other staff members. For their skilled work in preparing the photographs and offering advice, I am extremely grateful to Roy Flukinger, Linda Briscoe-Myers, David Coleman, Barbara Brown, Pete Smith, and Eric Beggs. The maps are the work of talented graphics designer, Layne Lundström. I thank him as well as Dave Holston of the Design Center at the University of Texas. Staff members of the Perry-Castañeda Library at the University of Texas, in particular interlibrary loan specialist Wendy Nesmith, were also helpful.

Ransom Center Director Thomas F. Staley initiated this book by suggesting its inclusion in the Ransom Center's Imprint Series. Kurt Heinzelman shepherded the book through to a completed manuscript, offering invaluable advice and support along the way. I thank them both extravagantly.

I express my sincere gratitude for their expertise and cordiality to the editors and staff at the University of Texas Press, especially Jim Burr, Leslie Tingle, and Sheila Berg. Finally, my thanks to Linda Webster for providing the index.

ON THE DIRTY PLATE TRAIL

INTRODUCTION
The Babb Sisters

Don't let this year make a damned fool of you next year.

OKLAHOMA PANHANDLE SAYING

Returning home from Denver and Leadville in 1879, Walt Whitman remarked that the plains of eastern Colorado and western Kansas impressed him more than the grandeur of the Rocky Mountains. He predicted a populous future for the region.[1] The Great Plains, Whitman wrote soon after the trip, would become "A newer garden of creation, no primal solitude, / Dense, joyous, modern, populous millions, cities and farms / With iron interlaced, composite, tied, many in one." Similarly, William Cullen Bryant's "The Prairies" (1850) envisions an "advancing multitude / Which soon shall fill these deserts." Early travelers responded diversely to the Great Plains, as Ray Allen Billington notes, ranging from semireligious awe to recoil against loneliness and isolation.[2] Such impressions were formed quickly, with little recognition of the variations in soil, climate, life-forms, and topology that exist in the Great Plains environment. Anyone with a deeper familiarity of this vast region, extending west from Illinois to the Rocky Mountains and farther beyond to the Great Basin, would have known what makes the High Plains so different from the neighboring prairies to the east.[3]

In his classic study *The Great Plains* (1931), Walter Prescott Webb marks the ninety-eighth meridian that bisects Kansas and Oklahoma as a line marking semiaridity: to the west annual rainfall is less than twenty inches, defining a region that before Anglo settlement was devoted to grazing and hunting. The entire Great Plains, as Webb points out, is a comparatively level, treeless, and subhumid region.[4] These characteristics are intensified on the High Plains to the west of the hundredth meridian, where like a canted deck the plains tilt upward to join the Front Range of the Rockies. In the period from 1961 to 1990, according to the National Weather Service, the annual rainfall in the High Plains (elevation ranges from 3,000 to 5,000 feet) amounted to little more than eighteen inches. This is less than half of that received in the fertile prairies of eastern Nebraska, Iowa, and Illinois. Prevailing winds of

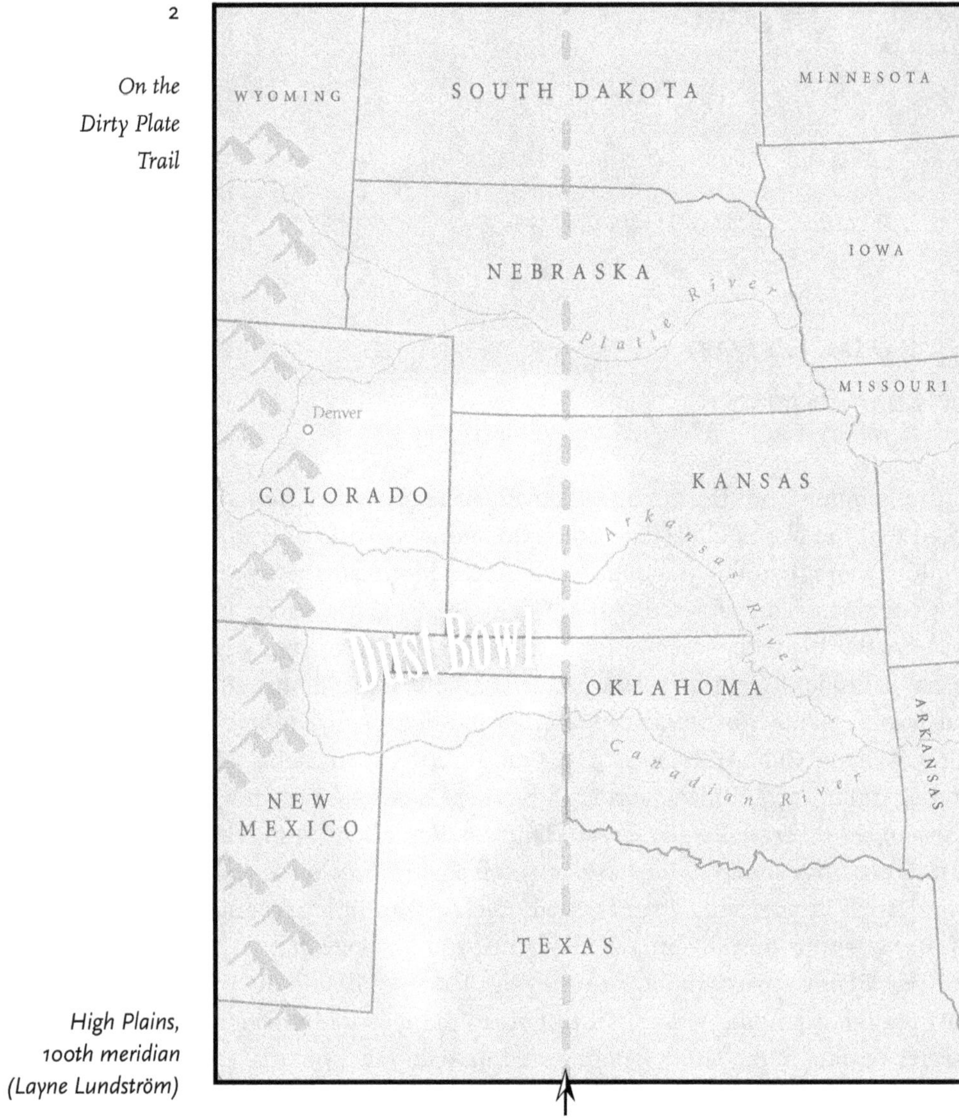

High Plains, 100th meridian (Layne Lundström)

relatively high velocity exacerbate the decrease in annual rainfall, driving terrible blizzards down the plains and scouring the earth in great dust storms. The few existing desiccated trees offer little shelter.

To Zebulon M. Pike, crossing westward in 1810, the High Plains appeared unfit for human habitation, an opinion reiterated by subsequent explorers such as Stephen Harriman Long of the U.S. Topographical Engineers, who coined the term "Great American Desert." This view was revised following the expedition in 1842 of John Charles Fremont, who saw opportunity for exploitation. Of a different opinion was John Wesley Powell, who, in his *Report on the Lands of the Arid Regions* (1878), cautioned against expansion. Environmental conditions, he argued, necessarily limit cultivation. Josiah Gregg, on the other hand, in *Commerce of the Prairies* (1844), promoted settlement. Cultivation, he said, would lead to rainfall. By 1875 farmers had begun to settle the grasslands where the Cheyenne and Kiowa tribes had hunted buffalo and ranchers grazed their cattle in summer. Yet an extended drought in the early 1890s chastened the prospect of agricultural development. A series of land acts intended to institutionalize settlement on the High Plains early in the twentieth century took into account the region's special conditions. Encouraged by new dry-farming technologies and some ten years of favorable weather conditions, settlers from eastern timber regions poured in as the High Plains were opened to homesteading.[5]

Among these new settlers was Alonzo Babb, a widower, who had homesteaded in Baca County, Colorado, in 1910 to escape personal grief and inhibit his drinking. Joining him several years later was his son, Walter, and daughter-in-law, Jennie, and their two daughters, Sanora and Dorothy. Disillusioned with the growth of small-town life in Oklahoma (representing, in his mind, commercial values and hypocritical morality), Walter sought a freer, simpler way of life. Although isolation held little attraction for them, wives dutifully followed their husbands to homesteads on the High Plains. What choice did they have?

Sanora Babb, born in 1907 in an Otoe Indian community in Indian Territory (Oklahoma), and her sister, Dorothy, born in Waynoka, Oklahoma, in 1909, spent their early adolescence in a dugout home on the High Plains of eastern Colorado.[6] Their father, Walter, a professional gambler and sometime baker, moved the family to Baca County in a hapless, ultimately disastrous quest for simplicity and independence. And perhaps Walter too, like his father, Alonzo, hoped to dry out from an addiction, in Walter's case, gambling. The broomcorn boom that attracted a new wave of settlers after a period of depopulation went bust soon after World War I. For weeks on end the Babbs' diet consisted chiefly of boiled Russian thistle with pepper; the family nearly starved. Their itinerant existence in the Otoe town of Red Rock, followed by the dryland farm in Baca County and the family's subsequent moves to Elkhart, Kansas, Forgan, Oklahoma, and finally to Garden City, Kansas, formed the Babb sisters' sensibility and nurtured their compassion for all living things. Sanora's childhood friends remember her as a smart, proud, spirited young girl who endured the humiliation and deprivation of the "dirt poor." They recalled her curiosity, passion for books, and outgoing disposition and were not surprised that she became a writer. Living in what was then known as "no-man's-land" (the Oklahoma Panhandle), Sanora was determined to write of the High Plains people, who at that time were without a literature and too new to the land to create a history.

Sanora Babb with Dust Bowl refugees

Ecological disasters occurring on the High Plains are associated in Babb's writings with broken dreams, human tragedies brought about by false expectations, speculation, and the restless demand for land. In this remote, harsh, dry land, Sanora and Dorothy created a life rich in the closely observed detail of nature and everyday existence. "We hung back," Sanora writes in her memoir, *An Owl on Every Post* (1970), "watching a large anthill, the great red ants hurrying carrying prey, sticks, enormous loads they put down and picked up again, moving in an orderly, inexorable way toward their destruction." The description might have served as a metaphor for the existence of the refugee dry-land farmers of the 1930s, picking cotton in California's Central Valley, whose story she tells in *Whose Names Are Unknown*, a novel written in

1939 but first published in 2004. Like the Brontë sisters sequestered in an English parson's home, the Babb sisters in their dugout home eight miles from Two Buttes, Colorado, imagined fictions that enhanced their lives of narrowed circumstances. Later, as a mature literary journalist, Sanora gave voice to these dryland people displaced from their High Plains homes by the bad times of the 1930s.

In the tradition of writers like Dreiser and Hemingway and contemporaries like Fannie Hurst, Martha Gellhorn, and Katherine Anne Porter, Babb apprenticed her literary career in journalism. In the early 1930s she turned to short stories and sketches published in little magazines that sprouted like seedlings across the country while the overall economy, it seemed, showed no sign of recovery. Through publication in literary magazines Babb became friends with other young writers in Los Angeles, where she had moved in 1929, including William Saroyan, John Fante, Tillie Olsen, Carlos Bulosan, and John Sanford, all of whom published their early work in the same magazines.

Journalistic experience and a compassionate social consciousness were Sanora's preparation for documenting labor conditions in Gallup, New Mexico, and the construction of Boulder Dam, Nevada, in the early 1930s. Her political education had taken root in the Populist-Socialist traditions of Oklahoma and Kansas. In Los Angeles she came into contact with progressives committed to working-class social justice. Returning in 1937 from a trip to the USSR, where she studied theater productions in Moscow and Leningrad and traveled extensively, Sanora rejoined the "dusted out" dryland farmers among whom she had grown up. Forced off their land by dust and low crop prices and bankrupted in their businesses, thousands of the dispossessed from farms and small towns migrated to the western states. Sanora helped to set up and run government-sponsored camps for the refugees, moving with them as they worked the harvests north along the "dirty plate" trail of Highway 99, from early winter pea picking in the Imperial Valley to fruit harvests in the San Joaquin Valley, then farther north to the Feather River, finishing with fall cotton picking in Kern County.

The titles given the refugees and their origins—"Okies" and "Dust Bowl"—were misnomers. The dispossessed came from diverse regions of the Midwest and Southwest and were widely varied in class status, education, and attitudes. Of this diverse population, the High Plains people represented a fractional element of sturdy, independent, literate farmers, most of whom had not known the degraded conditions of sharecropping and hired labor or did not share the religious and racial biases common among the Okies from Arkansas and eastern Oklahoma. They were not, in short, the illiterate, superstitious folk portrayed derisively in the right-wing press or empathetically in Steinbeck's *Grapes*

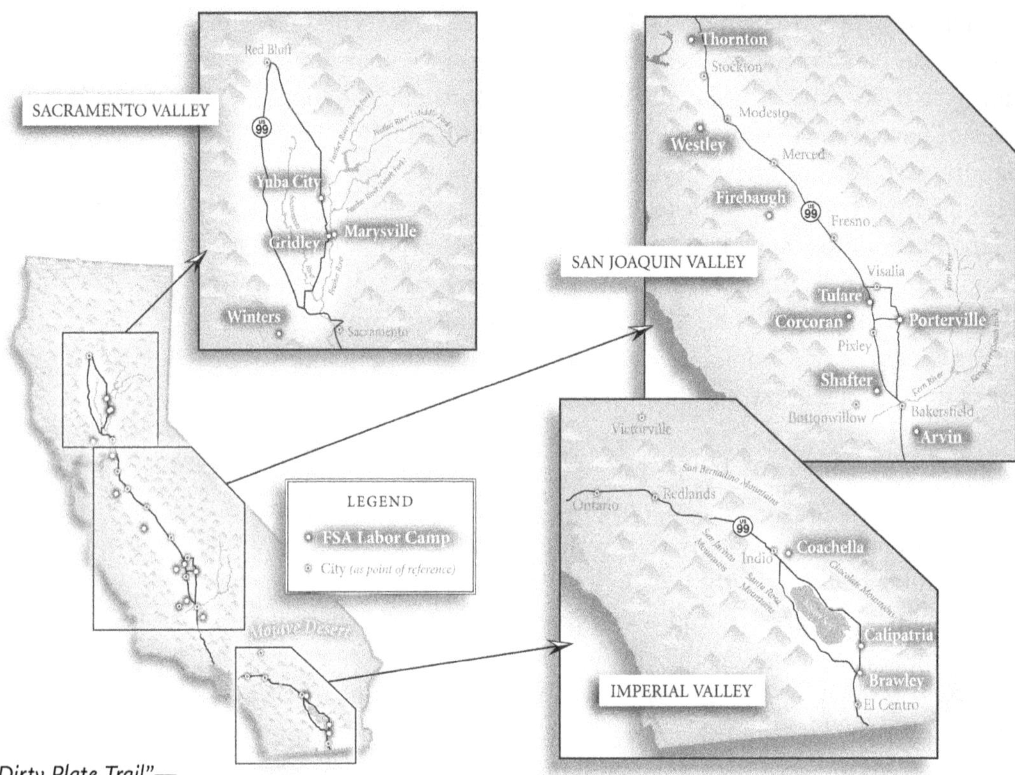

"Dirty Plate Trail"—old Highway 99, with sites of FSA migrant labor camps (Layne Lundström)

of Wrath (1939).[7] Fearful of the newcomers' burden on their schools and health facilities, townspeople expressed resentment, fueling exclusion and prompting political action groups intent on curtailing migration. The refugees were stigmatized as outsiders in spite of the fact that they looked like the local people, spoke the same language, shared the same national, religious, and ethnic identity, and observed similar customs. Far from lazy "white trash," most of the refugees were willing to work long hours in order to reestablish themselves and put down roots. Within a few years most were able to establish themselves as permanent settlers in better-paying occupations.

Deeply socialized by the same postfrontier conditions that historically had fostered individualism and conservative politics, Babb reconnected with her childhood and youth in the tent camps and along the dirt roads in California where new arrivals squatted in their cars until they found work. Initiating cooperative arrangements for their children's education and health, organizing labor demonstrations for better conditions, and recording the refugees' stories, she was able to enter the intimacy of the dispossessed farmers' lives and share their experiences. These experiences, together with what she knew of the dryland farmers growing up in the Dust Bowl, furnished material for her novel *Whose Names Are Unknown.*

The present volume collects Sanora's 1938–1939 field notes, including fragments, reportage, and short stories drawing on the same material. Dorothy, a gifted amateur photographer, recently graduated from the University of California, Los Angeles (UCLA), visited Sanora in the fields, bringing two cameras with her. Quite by accident amateur photographers sometimes become witnesses to events of historical significance. George Nathanial Nash, a British army lieutenant and amateur photographer, assigned as an interpreter on a British mission to Petrograd in 1917, found himself in the midst of a revolution and recorded it in memorable images. Likewise, Paul Patrick Rogers, visiting Republican-held Spain in 1937 as a member of an international commission, took pictures of the war refugees, comprising an invaluable historical record. On her own initiative Dorothy decided to photograph what she witnessed in the fields and camps of the Central Valley. Nash, Rogers, and Babb were not professional photographers or photojournalists; yet their photographs, accidents of time and place, left an incomparable visual record that does not exist elsewhere.[8]

What distinguishes Dorothy's photos from those of professional photographers hired by the Farm Security Administration is the freshness and immediacy of the images made without self-conscious posing

"Okies"—refugee farmers

or searching for the decisive moment that might reveal some essential quality of suffering and endurance.[9] Dorothy and Sanora interpreted the refugees' conditions in a process of change, linked to the everyday, makeshift practices employed to transform them. Central to this recognition was the nature of class relations (as in Dorothy's photos of the growers' homes) and the social struggle, which derive from historically specific modes of appropriation and domination. If Sanora, as storyteller, focused on individual personal stories, Dorothy was drawn to imaging not only the people but also the modes of production particular to the system of landownership and agriculture. Together Sanora's writings and Dorothy's photos represent a unique look into the lives and conditions of the refugees quite distinct from either Steinbeck's 1939 novel or the work of the FSA photographers.

The FSA's object in hiring professionals such as Dorothea Lange and Arthur Rothstein was not only to preserve a historical record but also to publicize the conditions afflicting the refugees in the camps, as well the government's work in alleviating their misery. The FSA photographers went much further than documentation and publicity, and, in some notable instances, they created lasting works of art. From the perspective of social documentation, however, they risked sublimating the actual subjects—real people and personal narratives—into aesthetic artifacts, icons of suffering, deprivation, despair. Lange acknowledged that she spent as little as ten minutes with a subject, without learning the person's name or knowing his or her story, taking numerous shots from which a selection was then made. The photos reveal much, at least insofar as they universalize the condition of homelessness and privation. Lange, Rothstein, Russell Lee, Walker Evans, and others created humanistic works of art, testimonies to the human condition, but silent on the actual names and individual histories that might interest social historians or, indeed, writers such as Sanora Babb.

Apart from the film quality, the chief difference between the Babb sisters' documentation of the refugees and the artistic achievements of the FSA photographers has to do with Sanora's artistic vision and, one might say, her personality. Like Sanora's writing, Dorothy's photos reveal an unmediated, personal encounter with her subjects, people with names and individual stories known to both Sanora and Dorothy, who were familiar figures among the refugees. Learning that the two sisters had grown up on a dryland farm on the High Plains, the refugees accepted them like their own, dropping any of the suspicion with which they viewed "outsiders." While it is not a criterion of value in writing or photography to have known one's subject in an experiential way, it represents a difference marking the choice of subject matter and actual recording of image or field note.

Sanora is in the company of writers—Maxim Gorki and Charles Dickens come to mind—shaped by cruelty and hunger and distinguished by their compassionate understanding of the outcasts and the poor. Dorothy fared less well in her life and work than Sanora. Dependent on her older sister, she became semireclusive, lacking the drive to engage her considerable artistic abilities in a professional capacity. A profoundly relational and life-affirming person, Sanora viewed suffering and privation as "here and now" circumstances deserving action rather than as abstract issues presenting spiritual dilemmas. This perspective she shared with many other literary radicals of her generation who wrote about unemployment, strikes, police brutality, homelessness, and dispossession for little magazines and progressive newspapers. All of them wrote, as Richard Wright said, "out of what life gives us in the form of experience."[10]

In the extensive studies of the Great Plains people displaced from their farms, jobs, and businesses in the 1930s, insufficient attention has been given to distinctions among regions, as if the people forced to leave their farms and businesses formed a sole constituency, uniform in their education, origin, social class, and aspirations. Sanora Babb's work underscores important regional differences characterizing the High Plains that reside in climate, soil, occupation, economic class, gender, and race. In giving voice to the voiceless and recording the tragic history of their dispossession, Babb locates a space that is at once physical, emotional, social, political, and temporal and that connects historical event and physical reality. As literature it transcends these limitations, ordering the emptiness, loneliness, and vastness of the High Plains through acts of the imagination. The challenge for a writer is to find the aesthetic means to give the unbounded, featureless physical space of the Great Plains artistic expression. The passionate vision of Willa Cather's Alexandra Bergson wresting wealth from the land in "the Divide" of southeastern Nebraska; the bitter struggle of Mari Sandoz with her tyrannical pioneer father in the upper Niobrara country; the brooding figure of Beret Hansa in O. E. Rölvaag's *Giants of the Earth*—all situate a distinct space that requires ordering acts of the imagination to evoke.

Each of these writers shapes individual memories into a larger collective memory—indeed, helps to create it—functioning both as cultural history for a community of people linked by the circumstances of place and time and as transmitter of memory to a community of readers unfamiliar with these circumstances. When individuals who experienced events of significance no longer exist to recall them, their words dying with them, when a memory has become a subject for study and the events seem foreign, then writing and photography serve as a means to preserve what otherwise would be lost. Drawing on memories of Baca County and the Oklahoma Panhandle and fusing these with her experiences in the tent camps and fields of California's great valleys, Babb made her notes and fashioned her published work. This work, I argue, is a constituent in constructing the cultural memory of the High Plains people and their migration to the western valleys. As a communicative process it achieves continued evocation through publication and readership.

Cultural memory in turn situates a place by evoking what is significant from the past so that the sum figuratively constitutes a site.[11] Such a site of memory is constituted by the tragedy of the dispossessed farm families in the 1930s, whose collective memories are commemorated in expressions such as "Okie" and "Dust Bowl migration." Commemorative events such as the annual Dust Bowl Days at Weed Patch Camp in California's Central Valley reenact the cultural memory of actual historical events and the people who participated in them.

The artistic legacy of the FSA photographers, Steinbeck's *Grapes of Wrath*, and the Babb sisters is part of the process of transmission involving repetition and transfer. Dorothy's photographs and Sanora's texts offer an alternative perspective on the iconography of dispossession and migration that is embedded in the national consciousness as the Dust Bowl exodus. Moreover, they serve to reframe and illuminate questions having to do with farm labor and immigration policies today. One clear lesson is the permanence of mass flows of labor as a fundamental constituent of food production in an industrialized agricultural system that increasingly is controlled by corporate ownership.[12]

The economic and environmental conditions that we associate with the Dust Bowl are unlikely to occur again in quite the same way or with the same human cost. Yet our food is still planted and harvested by workers who come from elsewhere, crossing national borders as they did before the great internal migration of the 1930s. This silent army of seasonal laborers from across our southern border has its own storytellers and iconography. We are wise to give them our attention, for their stories too redeem the hopes of the past and inscribe the cultural memory of the future.

1 THE DIRTY PLATE TRAIL

Workers of the Western Valleys

In the presence of extraordinary actuality, consciousness takes the place of the imagination.

WALLACE STEVENS

For nearly a century farmers and villagers in Mexico have left their homes for "el norte" to pick peas, cotton, and grapes and gather oranges from citrus trees in California's Imperial and Central Valleys. Of the estimated 5.3 million unauthorized Hispanic workers living in the United States (in 2004), a number increasing yearly by about 500,000, many have become legal residents as a result of periodic amnesties such as the 1986 Immigration Reform and Control Bill. Without counting their families, about 1.2 million of 2.5 million wage-earning farmworkers reside in California at present.[1] Across the nation a labor army of seasonal workers, mainly Latinos, harvest the crops, silent and enduring. From the early days of statehood to the present, the main source of farm labor in California fields has been migrant workers of foreign origin, a seemingly inexhaustible reserve of cheap labor harvesting our food. Like immigrants from elsewhere, the Mexican workers who have chosen to remain are making changes in their new homeland. In small towns throughout California's agricultural valleys, they own or manage businesses and service companies. People of Mexican origin—both seasonal workers and permanent residents—continue to play a central role in making California's valleys the gardens of America.[2]

Despite their indispensability, migrant farmworkers have remained an invisible labor force in the United States. Occasionally a brilliant labor leader such as César Chávez gains national attention or a report of migrants perishing in a locked freight car appears in the news. But, as Camille Guerin-Gonzales points out, little has effectively changed for the seasonal farm laborer (138). Ninety-eight percent of pickers in the raisin fields around Fresno today, according to David Vaught, are Mexican migrants (188), impelled to emigrate because of impoverished conditions in their homeland. The migrant labor system seems best suited for the growers. The sheer number of unskilled and uneducated workers, most without a command of English, keeps wages relatively

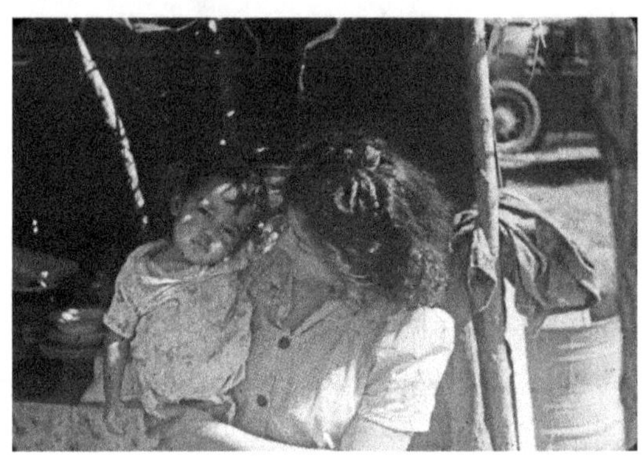

TOP LEFT:
Mexican migrant workers in camp

TOP RIGHT:
Mexican migrant worker with guitar in camp

ABOVE LEFT:
Slim Quinteros, labor organizer

ABOVE RIGHT:
CIO camp, Mexican migrant worker with child

low. The problems of legal residency are eliminated because harvesting requires no permanent labor force. Further, under current immigrant law an employer is permitted to hire "undocumented aliens," although the same law exposes undocumented persons to the threat of deportation.[3]

Labor organizations such as the United Farm Workers have done much to improve their lot; nonetheless, in some instances the conditions of farm labor in California have scarcely improved. Several years ago the *New York Times* reported on the squalor of Mexican fruit pickers near Mattawa who were living in tents on the banks of the Columbia River.[4] In rich coastal farmland near Lompoc, California, the incidence of respiratory diseases has reached epidemic proportions, a result of pesticide drift. Little attention, however, was given to the health effects on the immigrant field workers.[5]

For a brief time in the 1930s and early 1940s dispossessed Anglo migrants, together with a small number of blacks, did the main harvesting work of the western valleys.[6] A short-lived interlude in America's history of seasonal farm labor, the Dust Bowl exodus quickly became a symbol of all that went wrong in the Great Depression. In the period between 1935 and 1940, some 350,000 impoverished people, called "Okies," fled their homes in desperation and headed for California.[7] In the long history of migrant farm labor in the American West, the so-called Dust Bowl migrants occupy a disproportionately large space in history writing and cultural memory. The reasons for this now seem quite clear: the spectacle of mass dispossession ran counter to Jeffersonian ideals of independence on lands in the West. Families suffering privation and humiliation, publicized in photographs, film, and newspapers, shocked the nation. The ensuing politicization of the refugee crisis stirred up a publicity machine that lodged the inaccurately titled Dust Bowl migration in the public's mind and imagination. It continues to exist, reenacted through, art, literature, and commemorative ceremony.

Of the diverse collection of people from Oklahoma, Texas, Arkansas, Kansas, and other Great Plains states, fewer than 5 percent were actually Dust Bowl farmers.[8] Most of the refugees from Oklahoma, for instance, came from the central and eastern regions of the state, in particular the southeastern cotton belt. These were mainly tenant farmers and sharecroppers, whose speech and manner were identified erroneously with the Dust Bowl, or dryland, farmers. The stream of refugees also included tradesmen, teachers, lawyers, and small business owners, brought low by the economic depression. Some returned to their homes when times improved, but most remained in their adopted states, making a new life for themselves and their families.

Okie descendants today number some four million, one-eighth of California's population. The plains farmers were not the first white seasonal workers in California fields; "fruit tramps," as they were called, had followed the harvests for decades. Yet these harvest hands were relatively few. Until a flood of dispossessed Anglos, together with a small

CIO camp, Mexican migrant workers

number of blacks, took their place in California's fields, the conditions of seasonal farm work failed to attract national attention.[9]

The history of seasonal farmworkers in California reaches back to the latifundia of the Spanish colonial period. By the end of the 1920s, Carey McWilliams points out, "the industrial character of California agriculture was firmly established; they were like "factories in the field."[10] Following fierce labor conflicts in the Imperial and San Joaquin Valleys in the early 1930s, culminating in a reign of terror in July 1934 in the Santa Clara Valley orchards, large growers began to view foreign-born seasonal workers, with their traditions of labor militancy, as liabilities. Many were denied work; some were deported. In addition, land reform in Mexico slowed the influx of seasonal workers. When dispossessed farmers and small-town dwellers began to arrive in increasing numbers following the terrible droughts of 1933 and 1934, growers saw an opportunity to hire them in place of troublesome Mexican and Filipino workers. The desperate farmers were willing to accept any wage at first; moreover, most had no experience in collective bargaining.

The Dust Bowl exodus catalyzed a deep fission in the country's social consciousness. Initially welcomed by the growers, the refugees stream-

Dust Bowl refugee children

LEFT: *Dusted out farmers*

RIGHT: *Home on wheels (tent on flatbed truck)*

ing into California in overwhelming numbers were soon viewed as a scourge, an unwelcome burden on county tax rolls and state social agencies. Divisions appeared. On the one side were those who viewed the farmer-refugees as luckless failures, a threat to community life and budgets. On the other side were those who saw them as victims of drought and economic failure who deserved help. National disgrace or national calamity—this great internal migration of Americans, many descendants of early pioneers, was a tragic chapter in American history. The Dust Bowl and the Okies have become familiar references through Farm Security Administration photographs such as Dorothea Lange's iconic "Migrant Mother" and Steinbeck's novel *The Grapes of Wrath*. They embody a particular American experience in which the counterpart of historical reality is imaginary representation occupying the collective memory of American people over generations.

Every October in California's Central Valley, where many of the dispossessed settled and eventually became part of existing communities or started new ones such as Little Oklahoma, festivals such as Dust Bowl Days commemorate the dusted-out farmers of the 1930s who loaded their families and bedding in overburdened vehicles and headed west. Okie old-timers and descendants who are attached to family memories of the Dust Bowl diaspora gather annually at Weed Patch, a tiny housing settlement located in cotton fields near Arvin. Formerly an FSA labor camp for dispossessed Okies, Weedpatch migratory labor camp—renamed Sunset Migrant Labor Camp—is now a seasonal home for some one hundred thirty Mexican American migrant farm laborers who harvest fruit in the irrigated fields of the valley for half the year and then leave for work elsewhere or return home. Others who have permanent visas remain; their children and grandchildren join the growing Latino population in California (and elsewhere).

The crisis of dispossessed Anglo and black farmers passed with the ensuing wartime economy that provided jobs in aircraft factories and shipyards. Most of the farmer-refugees left the fields for better-paying

Weed Patch Store, near Arvin FSA camp

work; some returned to their homes in the Great Plains and southern states. "Weed Patch" is a commemorative name now; and the Dust Bowl exodus itself has a place in the nation's collective memory.

The personal stories of impoverishment, sickness, insecurity, and survival, recorded by contemporary health workers and journalists, form a historical narrative that the Dust Bowl refugees unashamedly recount.[11] The tragic dispossession of Americans from the Midwest and the Southwest, the largest *internal* migration within a five-year period in American history, has become a memory site, in which suffering and loss are dignified, indeed commemorated, as a historic occasion of resilience and survival.

Farmer or Worker?

The Dust Bowl refugees were slow at first to organize collectively. In their minds unions were for urban factory workers. It was long an aim of the left to join farmers and factory workers in common cause for labor. But the dispossessed farmers dreamed of owning their own farms in order to become, in a sense, independent businessmen, perhaps even employers. Hispanic farmworkers, on the other hand, were familiar with collective labor activity; it was central to the Mexican Revolution. Nonetheless, they were reluctant to organize north of the border until the formation of the Confederación de Uniones Oberas (Confederation of Workers' Unions) in 1927, with twenty locals.[12] This example—organizing unskilled workers—attracted the attention of Communist Party of America (CPA) organizers from the Trade Union Unity League (TUUL). Ensuing Party-led strikes met stiff resistance from growers and California's justice system; key organizers were indicted and imprisoned under California's Criminal Syndicalism Act, a vestige of post–World War I antilabor legislation.

In 1932 the TUUL gave birth to the Cannery and Agricultural Workers Industrial Union (CAWIU), aimed specifically at California's farmworker population, most of whom at the time were Mexican in origin. Farmworkers had little bargaining power in the early years of the Depression; but with Roosevelt's election in 1932, the National Industrial Recovery Act emboldened CAWIU leaders to organize strikes for high wages, fewer hours, and the elimination of labor contractors. A series of strikes in the Imperial and San Joaquin Valleys (in 1933 and 1934) turned violent when vigilantes—"hired thugs" as the strikers called them—interceded against striking workers. Incidents of vigilantism and excessive violence brought public attention to the farmworkers' plight.

In the early years of the decade the Communist Party achieved notable success despite its small membership. Hoping to create a revolutionary vanguard, Party activists organized sharecroppers, textile workers, and miners, staged hunger marches, founded unemployed councils, fought white supremacy in the South, removed racial barriers in labor and the arts, and were instrumental in bringing about labor reforms. The Party in California received support from intellectuals and activists such as Lincoln Steffens and Ella Winter, wealthy patrons such as Noel Sullivan, and film stars such as James Cagney.[13] Yet its confrontational methods were often counterproductive, for example, in the San Joaquin Valley cotton strike in October 1934. Vigilantes and hired gunmen met the strikers in a series of violent conflicts during which the police arrested two key Party organizers, Pat Chambers and Caroline Decker.

The confrontation between growers and workers, resulting in the deaths of three strikers at Pixley, attracted national attention through newspaper coverage. The publicity resulting from the strike and subsequent events, including the trial of the accused organizers, pressured the state and the federal government to intervene. It also attracted the interest of University of California social scientists Paul Taylor and Clark Kerr, who, along with an attorney named Carey McWilliams, were soon to play a critical role in shaping migrant worker policy. Taylor's reports, in which he teamed up with Dorothea Lange, and McWilliams's newspaper articles, leading to his 1939 study of migratory farm labor in California, *Factories in the Fields*, enraged growers, fueling bitter disputes between progressive and conservative elements. Later, as head of California's Division of Immigration and Housing, McWilliams was involved in the struggle between the U.S. Senate's La Follette Committee and the House of Representatives' Dies Committee on Un-American Activities. It was significant of the times that two books dealing with contemporary social questions—McWilliams's *Factories in the Fields* and Steinbeck's *Grapes of Wrath,* published within months of one another—were able to prompt inquiries on the migrant labor situation at the highest governmental levels.

Reluctant to engage in collective action, the farm families from the High Plains were used to making their own decisions and running their own affairs.[14] Moreover, the recently founded Congress of Industrial Organizations (CIO) was reluctant to organize farmworkers. Seasonal laborers moved on after harvest, complicating membership and organizational efforts. The growers felt emboldened following the demise of the CAWIU and the abortive strikes of 1934. Labor-management relations were tipped in favor of the growers when the refugees began to arrive in large numbers.

Yet the sheer numbers of refugees pushed their plight into the national spotlight; and the desperation of their situation led them to look for unfamiliar solutions, such as a labor strike. A series of strikes in 1934, from which Steinbeck drew material for *In Dubious Battle* (1936), led the large growers to organize the Associated Farmers of California, Inc., whose political power extended to the state legislature. By summer 1936 more than 86,000 refugees from the drought states had entered California; and two years later an additional 120,000 had arrived. Near-

BELOW LEFT: *Strike committee, Tulare and Kings strike*

BELOW RIGHT: *Strike picket line ("Come out, Scabs")*

BOTTOM LEFT: *Picket sign: "Come out, Boys. Help make your wife and children a living. What a husband that will work his wife in cotton for 80 cents per hour."*

BOTTOM RIGHT: *Memorial service, Pixley strike victims*

Peaches, Calpak orchard, Visalia

ly half a million refugees, it is estimated, took part in the exodus to the western states. The power of the large growers revealed itself plainly in the Salinas lettuce strike of 1936. Sheriff and deputies, local police, vigilantes, and company-paid thugs gathered to protect strikebreakers and to crack the heads of protesting Okies. The violence brought unfavorable publicity to large growers and corporate farmers such as Miller & Lux, the Tagus Ranch, and Di Giorgio Fruit Corporation; packing companies such as Libby, McNeil & Libby; and the giant landowner Pacific Gas & Electric, which contributed heavily to the Associated Farmers.[15] This time the strikers were predominantly Anglos, not Latinos. And the Fruit and Vegetable Workers Union organizing the strike was not run by the CPA, which made it easier for journalists to give favorable press coverage to the strikers. Moreover, newspaper reporters who ventured near were beaten by thugs. Impugned and scorned by locals as subhuman Okies, the farmer-refugees were winning sympathy statewide. Protest meetings were held. Hollywood stars raised money, and some brought presents and food to the camps.[16]

Now the Roosevelt administration became interested, prodded by the energetic Rexford Tugwell, architect of the National Relief Administration. Beginning in 1933, the Soil Erosion Service, a newly initiated agency of the Interior Department, conducted erosion control demonstrations such as planting tree belts. Later this agency became the Soil Conservation Service under the Department of Agriculture.[17] Under Henry Wallace's leadership, the Department of Agriculture had a significant role in New Deal programs. After passage of the Jones-Connally Farm Relief Act in 1934, for instance, the government purchased livestock on drought-ravaged western grasslands. This was followed by the Taylor Grazing Act, which withdrew land from the public domain in order to provide grazing districts. The government purchased marginal farmland and resettled families in efforts to ease the devastation of land and human livelihoods. Mistakes like the farm relief programs enacted in 1933 by the Agricultural Adjustment Act (AAA) were corrected. A great transformation was under way, a dramatic speedup in the shift from a predominantly rural society to an urban one that introduced political divisions and social disruptions like nothing the country had ever experienced. By the end of the 1930s many of these dispossessed farmers, at heart social conservatives prizing individual liberties and self-reliance, assumed new roles as industrial workers in factories tooling up for war.

Refugees in Their Own Land

"Burnt-out" farmers from Oklahoma, Arkansas, Texas, Kansas, and a half dozen other midwestern states crossed into California along U.S. Highways 66, 60, and 80, their jalopies burdened with bedding, dirty-faced kids, and suitcases tied to the running boards. They were a mixed people, many of them old-stock Americans, progeny of earlier frontier migrations, representing different origins, education, and status. There were sharecroppers from southeastern Oklahoma—Steinbeck's Joads—and Arkansas, homesteaders from the High Plains, tenant farmers from Oklahoma, and a considerable percentage of people who had lost their farms through foreclosure or abandoned them in desperation.[18]

The dryland farmers of the High Plains were generally literate, self-reliant, frugal people whose aim was to keep their families intact and eventually start a new farm. Former homesteaders, or children of homesteaders, many dryland farmers had owned equity in their farms. But when crop prices fell after World War I, they were forced into tenancy—or foreclosure. Subsequently, the combination of Depression and drought in the 1930s brought them down the economic scale yet another notch to become farm laborers and, finally, migrants.[19]

The manners and speech of the former tenants and sharecroppers of eastern Oklahoma and Arkansas were rough compared to those of the dryland farmers. Apart from their diverse origins, education, and occupations, all of those who had lost their employment and joined the trek west felt keenly the humiliation of their condition. To get off relief they had left their homes and gone to California.[20] But it was demeaning to accept the conditions of migratory labor, to be a people without status or voice; yet they generally met these conditions with a determination to

Loshope family, refugees from Arkansas

Dust Bowl girl

LEFT: *Games, FSA camp*

RIGHT: *Halloween in an FSA camp*

endure and see better days. Now they were a declassed homeless people, their rights as American citizens ignored and violated; an uprooted folk for whom the American creed of work and success had failed. Shattered was their pride as citizens, inheritors of Jeffersonian ideals. For them, California's golden vistas were the pitiless glare of sun-starched fields, where they picked cotton and peas for pittance wages and suffered discrimination and scorn from resident Californians who viewed them as intruders, a freeloading, disreputable rabble.[21]

Following the seasons, the refugees worked the harvests northward, beginning in the pea and winter lettuce harvests of the Imperial Valley in January and February and continuing through the Central Valley's long cotton harvesting season to the apple orchards of Oregon and Washington. Farm owners provided temporary quarters in one- or two-room shacks for some; others squatted in tents on private land set aside by the owners—or simply parked in a ditch and slept next to their cars. Yielding to pressure from the Associated Farmers and other interest groups, California's State Emergency Relief Administration (SRA) refused relief payments and opposed federal interference, which would only invite more refugees to the state. Yet the refugees' living conditions had become a sore point for the state and the federal government; strikes, demonstrations, and the left press kept the refugees' plight in the public eye. Pressure was on for reforms. It came finally on the heels of the failed Agricultural Adjustment Act. In spring 1935 the Roosevelt administration issued an executive order establishing the Resettlement Administration (RA). Within two years, the RA was moved to the Department of Agriculture, where, in an act of Congress (Bankhead-Jones Farm Tenant Act), it became the Farm Security Administration.[22]

The California State Emergency Relief Administration had set up temporary shelters for refugees the previous year in Visalia. In spring 1935, inspired in part by the Taylor-Lange reports, the SRA's federal counterpart (Federal Emergency Relief Administration [FERA]) began construction of model camps, in part to set a higher standard for the

Refugee farmer and guitar, FSA *camp*

Refugee workers repair their cars

growers, who might see economic benefit from better-housed workers. By year's end the Marysville and Arvin camps were housing refugees in tent camps with sanitation facilities, laundries, health dispensaries, and recreational halls. The camps were soon turned over to the RA, and in 1937 to its successor, the Farm Security Administration. By decade's end some forty-five thousand refugees found temporary homes in thirteen camps, a small fraction of the actual number who found temporary shelter in squatters' camps, in company shacks, and along the roadside. The RA/FSA "sanitary camps" were intended to demonstrate that when refugees were in clean and safe camps with laundry, sanitation, and community organizations pride and self-respect would return. Advocates argued that by removing the stigmas of humiliation and shame,

ABOVE LEFT: *Wash day in an FSA camp; wood floors for tents*

ABOVE RIGHT: *Refugee worker laying wood floor of tent home*

Laundry, FSA camp, Shafter

these men and women would be good workers and lessen the burden on the state's taxpayers. Yet detractors, including the powerful Associated Farmers and some congressmen, continued to protest federal aid. The camps, they said, would induce more people to migrate to California and provide forums for Communist agitation.

In fact FSA camps met only a fraction of the needs of the refugee field workers; moreover, Communism had little appeal to the mainly Anglo people who resided in them during the harvests. In the fields were a relatively small number of blacks, working alongside whites. By 1938 the newly established CIO tent camps had begun to welcome black refugees and Mexican migrant workers.[23] The Mexican workers were concentrated primarily in the Imperial Valley, where they lived and traveled in family groups. They consisted mainly of returning residents from California, Texas, New Mexico, and Arizona, numbering fewer than 4 percent of the total migrants and refugees.[24] An even smaller fraction of migrants were Filipino, mostly single individuals.

OPPOSITE PAGE

TOP LEFT: *Tom Collins, FSA administrator*

TOP RIGHT: *FSA mobile office*

BOTTOM LEFT: *Tom Collins making calls*

BOTTOM RIGHT: *FSA camp, Shafter*

The living conditions for most field workers outside the FSA camps were generally lamentable. To find shelter in an FSA camp, on the other hand, meant in most cases potable water, a clinic for children staffed with a resident nurse, a nursery, a community hall, a laundry room, and tents with wooden platforms. In addition, portable camps, adapted from army mobile camps, were also built. The FSA camps ultimately saved the state and the federal government money. Yet FSA administrators came under constant fire from conservative forces opposed to New Deal programs, which they viewed as giveaways to the undeserving.[25]

A tireless, devoted FSA administrator named Tom Collins had set up the first camp at Marysville in 1935, under the RA. He continued to administer other camps, including Weedpatch in Kern County. In addition to offering shelter and health care, the camps under Collins's direction functioned as a social experiment in rudimentary democracy. Collins used the term "democracy functioning," or DF, to describe the practices of the camps. Refugees made decisions by a show of hands and implemented them in the practical affairs of governance. Campers' committees formed the governing body of each camp, much like a town council. Discipline, disputes, and law and order were under the purview of this governing body of elected officials, serving as a link to the FSA managers. Separate committees were set up to sponsor sports contests and entertainment, provide health care for children, and maintain cleanliness. Special women's committees were responsible for child care. In the Arvin camp the Good Neighbors Society organized a library and a sewing club. These functions were not unfamiliar to the displaced farmers and townspeople; they were the means they had used to bring local government and social-cultural amenities to the western plains.

The camps published their own newsletters with titles such as the *Tow Sack Tatler* and the *Weedpatch Cultivator*. They included chatty news of local happenings and hearsay that the refugees were used to reading in small-town papers at home. The dryland farmers had been independent freeholders; they valued socialized traditions of cooperation and neighborliness, unlikely constituents of revolutionary activity. Loath to organize into a union, the dryland farmers nonetheless had inherited traditions of populist protest against mortgage speculation, unscrupulous banking and railroad company practices, and corrupt legislators.

The Babb Sisters in California

When Sanora and Dorothy Babb first met with Tom Collins in the Imperial Valley in February 1938, the refugee situation had reached a critical stage, politicized by both progressives and conservatives. Activists, unions, and liberal newspapers welcomed the FSA and other federal

LEFT: *Sanora Babb (1938)*

RIGHT: *Dorothy Babb (ca. 1940)*

programs. Critics, however—principally the corporate landowners and large growers but also conservatives who viewed with alarm "Reds" promoting dangerous interventions alien to American ways—sought to undermine government interventions such as the FSA.[26] Dorothy stayed briefly, then returned to Los Angeles. Sanora remained, joining Collins in constructing and managing FSA camps. During the course of the next few months, Dorothy rejoined Sanora to photograph the refugees in the camps and fields.

Compassion for the homeless farmers together with the democratic character of the FSA camps attracted Sanora to join Collins. These were progressive ideals, and Sanora, who had taken a turn leftward since coming to California, was swept up by them, as were many other young people who were radicalized by unemployment and the perception that working-class people were scarcely better off than the dispossessed farm people. Sanora's organizational skills and sensitivity to people proved invaluable to Collins; moreover, she was a talented writer who recorded the refugees' stories while working alongside them. Collins encouraged Sanora to make field notes. Documentation served an additional purpose: it helped to make the case for further government funding.

Sanora and Dorothy knew hunger and insecurity from their hardscrabble childhood on the High Plains. Their father, Walter, a restless man with a quick mind and little formal education, was a baker by trade who preferred to earn his living as a professional gambler. Walter brought his fifteen-year-old bride, Jennie, from Kansas to Red Rock in

Indian Territory in 1905. Two years later Sanora was born. For a time the family lived in Waynoka, Oklahoma, where Dorothy was born in 1909. In 1913 Walter moved his family to his father's broomcorn farm in southeastern Colorado in a quixotic attempt to construct a free and independent life as homesteader.

The four years in a one-room dugout with no water well ended in failure; for weeks at a time there was nothing to eat but flour pancakes and molasses. Walter went back to baking and gambling, first in Elkhart, Kansas, then in Forgan, in the Oklahoma Panhandle, where, despite opprobrium as the "gambler's daughter," Sanora graduated as valedictorian of her high school class. Walter was not content in any place long. Sometimes he left town just ahead of the law, seeking refuge in an adjoining state until things cooled off. In 1924 the Babbs family moved to Garden City, Kansas, where Walter, renting a room in the first-class Windsor Hotel, engaged well-paid travelers in poker and faro. With his earnings Walter bought expensive clothes for Jennie and the two girls; then it was hard times again and growing separation between Sanora and her father that she traces in her first published novel, *The Lost Traveler* (1958).

Cloistered by penury and the disapproval they endured as daughters of a gambler, Sanora and Dorothy nourished their youthful lives with books, poetry, and dreams. Their talent as poets attracted the attention of the *Garden City Herald*'s editor, who hired Sanora to write local news (Sanora had graduated from the junior college in Garden City after a year at the University of Kansas; Dorothy attended Emporia State College). With this experience, together with Associated Press credentials that she had earned in Kansas, Sanora set out for Los Angeles in late summer 1929.

Freshly minted as a journalist, Sanora had hopes of landing work with a newspaper. But within a month the stock market went bust; few jobs were available for young female journalists. Unable to pay her rent, Sanora spent nights on a bench in Lafayette Park, along with dozens of other homeless job seekers, while filling temporary secretarial assignments during the day—when they were offered. By spring 1930 she had found secretarial work in the Warner Brothers building on Hollywood Boulevard, and soon she was writing scripts for radio station KFWB.

Leaving Emporia State College and a position as teacher in a one-room rural school in Kansas, Dorothy joined Sanora in 1934. She enrolled at UCLA, from which she graduated with a degree in English. Los Angeles was an exciting place for young writers like Sanora who were publishing their work in little magazines such as *The Midland, The Anvil, Trend, Clay, Windsor Quarterly, Hinterland, The Magazine.* These and other little magazines had an influence far beyond the size of their subscriptions. Alfred A. Knopf, Scribner's, Viking, Covici-Friede, and other publishers looked for new talent in them. They also served to connect young writers on the West Coast including Sanora, William Saroyan, John Fante, Harold Salemson, Harry Roskolenko, Carlos Bulosan, Tillie Olsen, and Meridel Le Sueur. Sanora's circle of new friends also included a young Chinese American cinematographer, James Wong Howe, whom she later married.

Salemson, former editor of the expatriate literary magazine *Tambour*, invited Sanora to the short-lived John Reed Club in Hollywood. John Reed Clubs in Hollywood, Carmel, Chicago, New York, Santa Fe, Indianapolis, St. Louis, and elsewhere attempted to draw writers and artists to working-class subjects, part of the CPA's interest in including cultural activity in its broader programs. Drawn to progressive causes, Sanora joined the Party, not for ideological reasons, she said, but because it seemed to be the only effective advocate for the poor and the homeless. Restless with the authoritarian structure of functionaries, in-fighting, and political orthodoxy, she eventually left the Party. Joining had been a matter of the heart, she said, but her mind rebelled.

In 1936 Sanora, along with three others, including Herbert Klein (aka Kline), editor of *Theatre Monthly*, traveled extensively in the Soviet Union, principally to attend a monthlong theater festival in Moscow and St. Petersburg. Sanora stayed on for several months, returned to Paris, and spent an additional year in London, where she worked for Claud Cockburn's *The Week*, receiving his dispatches from Spain during the Civil War.

These, then, are the main threads—early poverty, a compassion for outcasts and the downtrodden, an artist's sensitivity, and the existence of an activist progressive movement whose ideals found resonance with her—that joined in Sanora's decision to help the dispossessed farmers, the people she had known from earliest childhood.

The Dirty Plate Trail

During the winter and well into the fall of 1938, Babb and Collins walked the dirt roads of the Imperial Valley and farther north into the Central Valley to the Feather River north of Sacramento. They set up tent camps and provided supplies for newly arrived Dust Bowl refugees who slept in their overburdened flivvers and roadside ditches. The two FSA workers told the refugees about the FSA camps where they could bathe, receive medical attention, find shelter in tents with wooden floors (for $10 extra), enjoy the camps' social life, and participate in camp management. Confused, dispirited, hungry, and often disbelieving, the refugees needed guidance in the first few weeks of their arrival.

They refused anything resembling welfare. Given jobs, they would take care of themselves and their families. It was the spectacle of a proud, independent people who were robbed of their livelihood and subjected to slurs and exploitation that struck Sanora and Dorothy and spurred them to record their impressions.

Photography had interested Dorothy from an early age, when Walter had given her a box Kodak. Learning that Dorothy planned to visit Sanora in the fields, Howe, an acclaimed cinematographer by that time, furnished her with a Rolleicord camera, which she used in addition to her 35mm Leica. He shared a few ideas on still photography with her but believed that a photographer should find his or her own way. The refugees accepted Dorothy, as they had Sanora, despite their natural reserve against "outsiders," including journalists and professional photographers who sought the socially and politically explosive material provided by the plight of dispossessed Americans.

The route of the seasonal farmworkers was the "Dirty Plate Trail"—Highway 99—which took them from peas in the Imperial Valley to cotton in the San Joaquin Valley to peaches and prunes in the Sacramento Valley. Theirs was emotionally and physically exhausting work; the evidence lies plainly before us in the photographs that Dorothy made. In the evenings Sanora composed her sketches of the refugees and made notes in a journal. She began a novel titled *Whose Names Are Unknown* in which she reframed her observations and memories, sketched initially in reportage and short stories. Like Katherine Anne Porter and Martha Gellhorn, Sanora possessed a journalist's eye for detail and a lively literary imagination. Her approach to the "Dust Bowl material" was immediate, affective, and objective, without artfulness.

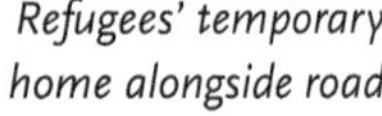
Refugees' temporary home alongside road

King family, refugee workers and musicians: Bill, John Henry (father), Charlie, Harlan, and Julie (l to r)

Whose Names Are Unknown draws on her intimate knowledge of dry-land farmers on the High Plains, their dispossession and attempts to reconstruct their broken lives in the migrant camps. She had seen the crude inscription addressed to those "whose names are unknown" on notices for eviction. The novel's title embodies the bitter fact that to the owners the field workers were nameless peons, expendable labor "units." In her documentation and fiction, Babb frames familiar names, places, and events in social and historical contexts.

The refugees, she perceived, were not hapless uninformed "Joads" who came late to a rudimentary kind of political consciousness. Most of them sought to reestablish themselves as farmers, tradesmen, or merchants. Radical speech fell on deaf ears; when conditions finally became intolerable, however, they organized strikes and welcomed visits from journalists, photographers, and Hollywood liberals who brought them clothing and toys for their children. The refugees tolerated these visits with quiet reserve, as people do when they will not be patronized but realize the political value of attracting attention to their plight.

Living among the refugees, Sanora devoted herself to the work of making the camps run, organizing the refugee women into committees to provide education and medical help, meeting with growers, and walking the roads to find stranded families. Local schools did not accept the children of the refugees; and sometimes hospitals would refuse to treat them. Collins and Sanora served as midwives numerous times, when women bore their children in tents on newspapers spread on the ground.

Most of the refugees arrived as families. The few bachelors tended to live in one section of the camp. The women baked on crude outdoor

TOP LEFT: *Harlan and Julie King*

TOP RIGHT: *Charlie and Bill King (r)*

ABOVE LEFT: *Charlie singing, Bill King with bass fiddle*

ABOVE RIGHT: *Beckenwirth family*

stoves and washed in tubs or in streams. Sanora recalled the King family from Arkansas, who played traditional Appalachian string music in the camps after work. They had appeared regularly on station KFPW in Fort Smith before losing their farm and moving to California. After work the men in the camps often gathered, sitting on the ground, discussing their plans and prospects. Music drifted across the camp from the Kings' tent: John Henry, playing the banjo, and his four children, Julia, on the fiddle, Harlan, on guitar, Charles, on mandolin, and Bill, on bass. On weekends Collins organized dances for the refugees, with music provided by the Kings and other camp residents.[27]

The Beckenwirth family had lived for a time in company-owned shacks. They were moved out when the harvest ended, forced to camp in their car until they found work again. Appearing in the photographs too are social workers such as Mrs. Evans, who investigated conditions for the state, and strikers picketing in the 1938 Kern County cotton strike.

Sanora was not a militant activist like Dorothy Ray Healey or Caroline Decker. However, when she learned that children were harvesting walnuts near Modesto without pay, she sought help from the United Cannery, Agricultural, Packinghouse and Allied Workers of America (UCAPAWA) in San Francisco. Founded by the CIO in 1937, the UCAPAWA picked up the fallen reins of the CAWIU, dissolved by the CPA two years earlier. Experienced organizers from the CAWIU joined the new union, yet the UCAPAWA experienced great difficulties, for instance, in competing with its rival, the American Federation of Labor (AFL), in the canneries. Moreover, the transitory nature of seasonal field work made it difficult to organize and collect dues. Some newly arrived refugees refused to join. In these early years when union officials were making their way tentatively among farmworkers, they turned down Sanora's request of organizational help with the walnut pickers. Undaunted she set about organizing a strike, and ultimately the workers' children were paid. During one strike, Sanora spent a night in jail, along with Dorothy Ray Healey, a Communist Party organizer, who had taken part in the 1934 lettuce strike in the Imperial Valley.[28]

Sanora was not inclined to impose her political views on the refugees. She knew they would make up their own minds in the face of unjust wage scales and unhealthy working conditions. Resistance—for example, spontaneous sit-down strikes in the fields—soon turned into organized CIO-led strike activity.

Strike organizers suffered great risks from police and thugs hired by farm owners. At a lunch counter in Porterville two men, hired to intimidate the strikers, sat down on either side of Sanora. "You'd better get out of town fast," they warned. "The last organizer who came through here—they found his body floating in a canal." When Sanora told Collins of the incident he advised her to leave immediately and relocate to another camp.

Dust Bowl Tales

Some of the selections in this collection appear for the first time in print, and most have not been reprinted since first appearing in little magazines. In one way or another they prepared the way for her first novel, *Whose Names Are Unknown*, published sixty-five years after its composition. The publication history of Babb's first novel is like her narrative of Dust Bowl refugees, a tale of hard luck and persistence. Tom Collins furnished his FSA field reports, to which Sanora contributed, to John Steinbeck, who visited Collins while researching *The Grapes of Wrath*. In the contested arena of federal funding for relief projects such as the FSA labor camps, it was important that the case be made to congressmen, who were deeply divided on the question. Moreover, Collins hoped that Steinbeck, renowned for his novel *Of Mice and Men*, would help him to get his own fictional narrative of the Okies into print.[29]

Steinbeck, as Jackson J. Benson, Jay Parini, and other biographers inform us, first turned his attention to the migrant workers in 1934, visiting the Imperial Valley in search of material and interviewing labor activists for *In Dubious Battle* (1936). His friend Francis Whitaker introduced him to the labor organizer James Harkins, who provided key material for the book. Through Whitaker, Steinbeck came into contact with a group of progressive writers and activists loosely gathered around Lincoln Steffens and Ella Winter in Carmel. Through these contacts, Steinbeck met George West, editorial writer for the *San Francisco News*, who asked him to write a series of articles on the Anglo migrants for his paper. Steffens's keen reportorial spirit, displayed in his muckraking work for *McClure's Magazine* early in the century, spurred Steinbeck's desire to observe actual events as source material for his writing. According to Benson, Steinbeck at first "remained emotionally uninvolved" with the misery of the migrants; his interest lay in finding material for a good story.[30] For novelistic reasons Steinbeck altered the details of strikes and conflicts that he observed, providing an open-ended conclusion to his tale so as not to appear to defend either the strikers or their antagonists. Steinbeck drew from key informants, such as the labor organizers Harkins and Shorty Alston, and prided himself on accuracy as befitting a realist writer. Yet he shaped his materials into a *roman à thèse* rather than a realist novel, dramatizing his theories on group-man, for instance, and the destructive elements of human nature that undermine constructive aims.

On a visit to the Central Valley in 1936, in preparation for the *San Francisco News* articles, Steinbeck met with Tom Collins through his contacts with the Resettlement Administration. After following Collins in his work as FSA camp administrator for several weeks, Steinbeck drew closer empathetically to the desperate conditions of the workers. The informal partnership with Collins bore fruit: Steinbeck's articles in the *News* brought pressure to bear on the growers to improve the conditions of the farmworkers. In researching his projected novel on the Dust Bowl refugees, Steinbeck drew heavily on the biweekly FSA reports, in which Collins recorded the speech idioms, personal narratives, and peculiar habits of the workers. These peculiarities of speech and manners led both Collins and Steinbeck to perceive the Okies as elemental *folk*. Steinbeck said that in his novel they were to be "more than people"; "[t]hey must be an over-essence of people" (quoted in Parini 252). Collins saw the Okies as participants in a social experiment of elemental democratic scope. Steinbeck, influenced by his marine biologist friend, Ed Ricketts, planned to invest in the figures of his new novel theories of group behavior showing individuals interconnected in a phalanxlike movement analogous to organic elemental matter.

Following the completion of *Of Mice and Men* (1937) and a trip to Europe, Steinbeck visited Collins again in the fields. The FSA headquarters had made arrangements for Collins to travel with Steinbeck for two weeks to tour a number of camps. Steinbeck's views had changed since *In Dubious Battle.* Now he hoped that his *News* articles would expose those who were responsible for the suffering he observed. Gathering the articles in a single volume, together with an additional piece, the Simon J. Lubin Society published them in a pamphlet titled *Their Blood Is Strong.* His growing fame put him in touch with the filmmaker Pare Lorentz, whose documentary methods Steinbeck admired and hoped to learn from. *Of Mice and Men* had brought him literary renown; Steinbeck felt obliged to conceal his identity during his travels with Collins. It was a better way to observe, he reasoned; moreover, hostile growers and their thugs were making threats against "outsiders."

In winter 1937–1938 terrible floods struck the Central Valley. Steinbeck spent ten days with Collins in mid-February helping him to collect stranded people and direct them to relief. During a short visit to Arvin several weeks later to prepare an article for *Life* magazine, Steinbeck met with Sanora and Collins. The three visited for most of the afternoon following lunch in a diner. Returning to his home in Los Gatos, Steinbeck immersed himself in the task of composing the manuscript of *The Grapes of Wrath,* a title his wife, Carol, fortuitously suggested. Viewing an earlier draft titled "L'Affaire Lettuceberg" as a failed attempt at satire, he destroyed the manuscript. Sanora remained in the fields into fall 1938, plotting her novel at night after work and making her notes. At roughly the time Steinbeck was nearing completion of his novel (October 1938) Sanora returned home to Los Angeles to write the draft of her own novel.

In late winter 1939 Sanora sent several chapters of her manuscript as a blind submission to Bennett Cerf, the legendary Random House publisher. Cerf paid Sanora's airfare to New York City, put her up at a hotel, and pushed her to finish the novel. Shortly before her arrival in New York *The Grapes of Wrath* was published by Viking Press. Within months it was a brilliant market success, much to Steinbeck's astonishment and far exceeding even Collins's fondest expectations. Cerf called Sanora into his office to tell her to put the manuscript away for a time. The present market, he said, would not welcome two novels on the same subject. Another Dust Bowl migrant novel might seem a poor cousin, given the spectacular promotion of Steinbeck's great achievement. Kyle Crichton, a Random House editor who had written satiric pieces for *New Masses*, took Sanora's manuscript around to other publishers, who responded similarly. Sanora was advised to wait; with time the subject would be valued for its "historical perspective."

The success of Steinbeck's novel overshadowed any other attempt to portray the refugees, no matter how well it was done. Babb's chances for early recognition were snuffed out. The lavish praise of her novel-manuscript by New York editors, including Maxwell Perkins of Scribner's, fueled her disappointment. Moreover, it was apparent that in the matter of narrative agency the Dust Bowl story had become gender biased. The subject demanded a male perspective; in the publishers' minds a woman's view carried less weight. Random House gave Sanora an advance to write another novel. She returned to her short story writing and eventually the novels *The Lost Traveler* (1958) and *An Owl on Every Post* (1971), both set in the High Plains.[31] Her Dust Bowl novel, *Whose Names Are Unknown*, finally appeared in 2004, to critical acclaim.

World War II created factory jobs for the refugees and conscripted many into the military. The focus was on winning the war; Depression-era subjects slipped quickly into forgetfulness. The public looked forward eagerly to postwar recovery and the bounty that would follow. Divisions sharpened on the left, exacerbated by the Nazi-Soviet pact. Rivalries and factional infighting weakened an earlier progressive consensus centered on justice and equity for the worker. After the war book publishers no longer looked to the little magazines in search of promising new authors of radical fiction. Informing, indictments, betrayals, blacklisting, and jail terms chilled or in some notable cases stifled artistic initiative. Artists, writers, and movie producers lost their jobs. In this "dark time," as Le Sueur called the Cold War era, creative people like Sanora felt safer abroad. She moved to Mexico in 1950 for a year, both to protect her husband's career and to escape the climate of fear that had turned friends and colleagues against one another in Hollywood.

Early penury, hardscrabble life on the High Plains, the insecurities of childhood as a gambler's daughter—all this might have embittered Sanora. It engendered, rather, a liberal sensibility, a reporter's eye, and a passion for life. Her writing ranges across a broad spectrum, from lyrical poetry to the texts of this collection whose aim is to look at life as it really is without dismissing the author's subjective involvement with the subjects. Obviously, in the emotionally charged circumstances of the Depression era a writer of Sanora's liberal sensibility and compassion would find little satisfaction as a dispassionate observer. Periods of tumultuous social change tend to foster realism; the power of what one experiences displaces fiction in its appeal to the imagination. True literary creativity, Albert Camus writes in *L'Homme révolté*, "uses reality and only reality with its warmth and its blood, its passion and its outcries. It simply adds something which transfigures reality" (428). Sanora fervently admired Turgenev and Tolstoy and, closer to her own time, Gorki and Sholokhov. She was drawn to the vision of Russian realists who not only attempt to portray life as it is lived but also criticize the conditions of existence in an effort to improve them.[32] She belonged to a generation of women journalists who turned reportage to creative uses in order to uncover deeper truths beyond appearances. A romantic by emotional inclination, Sanora nonetheless devoted her writing to fashioning a truthful picture of what she had observed and experienced. Romantic or realist, her greatest strength lay in seeing things clearly and telling them truthfully without artfulness or ideological slant.

Apart from its value in illuminating an important epoch in American history, the present collection provides many of the source materials that Babb reworked into *Whose Names Are Unknown*, and of which Dorothy's photographs are the visual counterpart. *Whose Names Are Unknown* portrays the dispossessed dryland farmers from an angle of vision quite different from Steinbeck's uprooted sharecroppers. Babb hewed close to testimonial evidence in novelizing what she knew firsthand of her subjects and their response to what they were compelled to endure. The novel's composition in the migrant camps gives it a freshness and an unornamented quality that reflect the material conditions of the refugees' everyday existence and the immediacy of Sanora's position with regard to the conditions and the people. Writing from *within* the lived experiences of the refugees placed her in the dilemma of a writer tugged by emotional involvement and at the same time determined to tell her story honestly. The sketches and statistics from her field journal became fully fleshed-out figures in short stories and novels. They are people we might have known as neighbors; indeed, in another time and place, we might have shared with them a similar destiny.

For both Steinbeck and Babb literature was best suited to embrace and give meaning to the refugees' great unfolding drama. So great in its scope and overpowering in its emotional impact on the sensitive observer was the subject that alone a naturalistic or journalistic treatment would have seemed inadequate. If in reading Steinbeck's novel the Dust Bowl refugees did not recognize themselves in the figures of the Joads, they did so in their plight. Biblical allusion and mythological structure universalize Steinbeck's narrative and lift the story from its specific historical contexts. *Whose Names Are Unknown*, on the other hand, remains firmly embedded in its historical contexts, exposing the forces driving events and interconnecting individuals and contemporary social-political transformations. The approaches of each are quite different, but the ambitious scope and human warmth of both novels give eloquent expression to the tragic calamity that actually occurred.

Texts and Photographs

In 1935 the Resettlement Administration set about publicizing the conditions of seasonal farm labor and the efforts of the government's refugee camps to alleviate the workers' misery. Within the newly established Information Division, Rex Tugwell, the RA's head, appointed Roy Stryker chief of the historical section. The RA's successor, the Farm Security Administration, also met heavy criticism. "Despite the transfer of the Resettlement Administration to the USDA [U.S. Department of Agriculture] and passage of the Bankhead-Jones Farm Tenant Act," Sidney Baldwin writes, "the claim of the FSA to legitimacy was tenuous and had to be continually reinforced" (269). Essential for continuance of its mission was public support, and that required public relations work. Baldwin notes that "the rhetoric *de rigueur* of the FSA was fairly consistent—the imagery and symbolism were rustic, an implicit faith in the virtues of poverty was pervasive, and the democratic mold of American society was invoked on every possible occasion" (270).[33] Stryker hired professional photographers such as Dorothea Lange, Russell Lee, Arthur Rothstein, and Walker Evans to document rural conditions throughout the country. These were gifted artists, who, in going well beyond the task of documentation, were able to order and alter the imaginative response to their subjects.[34]

Stryker was an able learner as well as manager of his talented artists; he perceived the powerful content of photos that turned the hardship of breadlines into human drama. At the same time, he instructed his photographers to inform themselves through study of the regions they visited—economy, geography, politics, culture, and so forth. Their approach was to focus on the subject matter in a problematic manner, underscoring underlying socioeconomic forces without suggesting solutions.[35] The result was some two hundred thousand photographs, many of which are permanent fixtures of art exhibitions and historical studies and retain their emotionally powerful impact on viewers.

"Migrant Mother," by Dorothea Lange, FSA, LC-USF342-T01-9058

Lange's close-ups of destitute people focus on human qualities that by virtue of their stark, parabolic quality make them personal and familiar, as if luck alone separates us from the subjects. Good art makes good propaganda, commented Lorentz, whose documentary films *The River* (1937), produced by the FSA, and *The Plow That Broke the Plains* (1936) are considered today masterpieces of cinematographic art.[36] Lange's photos are remarkable, William Stott points out, "especially when one considers how they were made: in the field, on brief acquaintance (she spent less than ten minutes with the "Migrant Mother" and didn't get her name), and of subjects aware what she was doing" (229). The FSA photographers used a great deal of film stock. Often several shots were made of a subject, and in some cases changes were made in the composition of the scene "in order to increase the graphic impact of a picture."[37] The FSA had facilities for film developing, but Lange insisted on doing her own developing, using methods she had learned from Edward Weston and Ansel Adams. And Russell Lee did some of his own developing while on site. Befitting their professionalism as visual artists, presentation and selection were essential elements of their work. The recropping of photographs, as Stott points out, removes the subject from the immediate historical context in order to represent "a figure in history whose hardship the viewer is incapable of easing—or a symbol of timeless sorrow" (230).

Selection and presentation might be viewed in some instances as manipulation of the subject for emotional effect, a charge made against Margaret Bourke-White by several of her peers, including Walker Evans, in her 1937 photo/text collaboration with Erskine Caldwell, *You Have Seen Their Faces*.[38] A similar complaint was directed at Lange in her 1939 sharecropper photos: a robust mother and smiling child belie the poverty, disease, and despair that was the southern sharecropper's lot.[39]

Lange, Evans, Rothstein, Lee, John Vachon, Marion Post Wolcott, Ben Shahn, Carl Mydans, and others were legendary figures when photojournalism discovered a broad readership in magazines such as *Life* and *Fortune*. Photography evolved quickly as a medium of social commentary. Yet the actual realities of the Depression era find inadequate and often misleading expression in words and photos. Scarcely better are statistical studies of the period, Lawrence Levine points out, adding that there is a tendency in the FSA images to view subjects as victims warranting our sympathy rather than, for example, as engaged in a struggle to maintain dignity and composure. "The urge," Levine argues, "to deprive people without power of any determination over their destiny, of any pleasure in their lives, of any dignity in their existence, knows no single part of the political spectrum.... The only culture the poor are supposed to have is the culture of poverty; worn faces and torn clothing, dirty skin and dead eyes, ramshackle shelters and disorganized lives. Any forms of contentment or self-respect, even cleanliness itself, have no place in this totality" (22–23).[40]

In Lange's justly famous photo-portrait of the unnamed "Migrant Mother" actual conditions experienced in the camps are raised to an aesthetic level of contemplation, abstracting misery as a human condition, tragic and unalterable. Babb's photographs, by contrast, are the work of a gifted amateur whose purpose was not simply to portray the refugees as victims of a failed economy and bad luck but also to explore the material causes of their condition and what they were doing about them. Her method was investigative in the manner of the Dutch filmmaker Joris Ivens, whose film of the Spanish Civil War, *The Spanish*

Earth, depicted not merely people fighting and dying, but *why* they were fighting and dying. Absent are stylized framing and selection. Their authenticity, one might argue, derives from the circumstances of their making.[41]

More than an amateur with two "German cameras," as she called the Leica and Rolleicord, Dorothy was a young woman of great intellectual ability, deep moral and political convictions, and droll wit whose reclusive tendencies frustrated Sanora, anxious that Dorothy become less emotionally dependent on her. Yet the sisters were close literary collaborators from the time they composed their first poems—Sanora urging Dorothy on and finding publishers for her work, Dorothy reading Sanora's work with a keen critical eye and suggesting subjects. Dorothy and Sanora's contacts with Filipino workers in Los Angeles and with leftist circles familiarized them in general ways with Marxist conceptions of economic crisis—notions such as class structure, the relations of production, and the formation of class consciousness.

In the tumultuous 1930s the tenets of historical materialism sallied forth from small cadres of Party theorists, attracting workers, intellectuals, and liberals eager to explain the causes of hunger and homelessness across the land. For Sanora (and other midwestern literary radicals) who had grown up with J. A. Wayland's *Appeal to Reason,* Debs's

FSA camp, mother and child

Socialist Party, and Emma Goldman's anarchism, Marxist discussions in Party circles seemed doctrinaire, less attuned to social realities than indigenous critiques of capitalism as they had known them. Exposing human conditions and causes of exploitation and class struggle through socially critical documentation had ample antecedents in American thought, so that literary radicals in the 1930s often embraced odd mixes of native radicalism and European imports. Socialist and Populist critiques had been household staples for the Babb sisters growing up in Oklahoma and Colorado. Their grandfather Alonzo subscribed to the Socialist newspaper *Appeal to Reason*, published in Girard, Kansas, and labor leaders such as Eugene B. Debs were familiar from political discussions at home. Walter's gambling associations with Wobbly harvest hands drew him to their freewheeling political views, codified compactly in the pocket-sized IWW songbook, whose preamble begins succinctly, "The working class and the employing class have nothing in common."

When Jacob Riis took his camera into New York City tenement slums his purpose was to catalyze action for reform. The short-lived Photo League established a center for documentary photography based on the

Beulah King

supposition that photography could affect social change.[42] According to Carol Shloss, Ansel Adams and other photographers associated with the League "wanted to bridge the gap between photographs taken with artistic intent and those taken for utilitarian purposes" (189). The "migrant problem," as it was known among social workers, demanded special critical tools that might reveal larger dislocations and inequities in the economy. Compassion alone was an inadequate response; it needed to be converted into action, or it would lead to indifference, apathy, and cynicism.

Dorothy's photos explore the workings of agricultural production: the workers, the owners, the living conditions, the conflicts, and the camp life. The subjects are in motion: men sitting on the ground conferring; women doing laundry and cooking on primitive stoves at the end of the day; trains bringing lumber for fruit boxes to the canneries; the owners' homes; the Kern County cotton strike of 1938; ancient vehicles in states of disrepair; the growers' self-promotion emblazoned on billboards; musicians like the King family; children at play; the government camp health clinics and laundry rooms—all unposed and unedited.

Several conclusions might be made regarding both Dorothy's photos and Sanora's texts. Professional constraints and administrative schedules allowed little time for FSA photographers to study the everyday lives of individuals and their work. Russell Lee, aided by his wife, Jean, frequently recorded the subject's name and location; but Dorothea Lange did not. Years later a diligent researcher located the subject of Lange's "Migrant Mother," Florence Thompson, living in Modesto.[43] Dorothy's photos, on the other hand, are labeled with names, places, and events. Among her subjects were the King family. The deep lines in the face of Beulah Elizabeth King sitting on a bed reveal the strain of a migrant mother's life, yet the neatness of her dress and amused, confident look belie a hapless victim. In reviewing more than two hundred of Dorothy's photographs, I find similar witnesses to hardship and the uncertainty of their situation, people who organize their lives, individually and collectively, play and socialize when they can, and bear their circumstances with patience and humor. This impression no doubt derives in part from Dorothy's choice of subjects but not altogether.

In summarizing, then, I suggest that apart from purely aesthetic considerations—the FSA photos are obviously superior in technical and artistic quality—the significance of Dorothy Babb's photographs is found in their laying bare the material and human conditions of dispossession. Moreover, they tend to be investigative and compassionate rather than emotionally compelling. Finally, they present an optimistic view of a sturdy people whom experience has toughened, not hardened or embittered.

Most of the refugees made it through the time intact, unashamed of having experienced it. The recollection of having endured with others a near-calamity drew them together, imparting a certain identity. In portraying the refugees' predicament, Sanora and Dorothy focused on the immediate conditions of its contingency. Their work serves to underscore this contingency in revealing it as the product of specific historical forces, partly to be mastered, partly endured. It deserves our attention and recognition for profilerating—to use the French philosopher Michel Foucault's criterion—these meanings.

An additional conclusion has to do with the status of the photographer and writer. Because they were sponsored by a government agency Lange and Taylor possessed a certain legitimacy among the migrant workers, who soon came to realize that the government offered protection from exploitative growers and their hired thugs and from discrimination by local residents. Yet Lange and Taylor remained outsiders, two professionals who stayed briefly and moved on to other locations, accepting the courtesy that interviewers generally receive in reporting and documenting. James Agee, in his (and Walker Evans's) famous study of southern sharecroppers, *Let Us Now Praise Famous Men,* wrestled with his observer status, the separate, hierarchical privileging of the writer-photographer. "What is mirrored by photography and by artists who have been influenced by it," Carol Shloss argues, "is, in this sense, American culture's tendency to organize itself hierarchically and to cloak interested motives in the language of equity while the true structure of privilege remains unnamed" (267).

By themselves Dorothy's photographs (and Sanora's writings on the refugees) might be viewed as products of hierarchical privilege—by the photographer viewing the subject through a lens, despite her "insider" status. But the combination of text and photo introduces a reciprocity and multiplicity of perspectives that, as Shloss suggests, is an aim of any democratic project. These photos belong to a vernacular tradition of photography that uncovers the conditions of their production and draws attention to their intent as historical documentation. They *expose* the contexts defining the particularities of their subjects, such as labor-management conflict, workers' organization and protest, conditions of agricultural production, unemployment, ethnic division, and migration.

Dust Bowl Exodus as Memory Site

Most vernacular photos disappear with their owner; the history of their making is seldom known, much less the identity of their subjects. Many of Dorothy's photos were made into black-and-white slides, probably for lecture purposes. Years later they turned up in a brown paper sack, where they resided until Sanora's nephew, Don Lee, drew my attention to them. We have a nearly complete record of the making of these photos, identification of the subjects, the circumstances of their production, the contexts in which the subjects were photographed, identification of the photographer, and biographical information.

The meanings and status of a photograph are related to its reception. The history of the FSA photos' reception on a national scale begins with their initial appearance in magazines such as *Life* and books such as Archibald Macleish's *Land of the Free* (1938). During the Cold War decades, critical realism and social content yielded to politically "safer" forms. The republication of these FSA photos, beginning in the early 1970s, in such volumes as *In This Proud Land* and *Let Us Now Praise Famous Men* signaled their recovery and renewed interpretation. This recovery is now expanding through attention to the work of lesser-known photographers such as Hansel Mieth, subject of a recent PBS documentary; Seema Weatherwax, whose work was recently exhibited in Santa Barbara; and Dorothy Babb, soon to be exhibited at the Harry Ransom Humanities Research Center at the University of Texas.

Altogether this great photographic legacy participates in a project of memory constructed from personal memories, documents, literature, film, and photograph and inscribed in a cultural memory site called "the Great Depression," linked to the metonymic image of the Dust Bowl. The experiences of uprooted farmers and displaced small-town folk are constituents of a national cultural memory that enshrines economic failure in myth, celebrating the lessons of deprivation and the virtues of toughness and resilience. This memory has evolved over time, shaped in great part by the work of the FSA photographers, Steinbeck's *Grapes of Wrath* and John Ford's 1940 film version, and headlined by the political controversies surrounding government programs of relief and aid.

Sanora and Dorothy were conscious that the dispossession and migration of hundreds of thousands of farmers to the western valleys was an event of great historical significance. If not for an editorial decision, Sanora's Dust Bowl novel might have helped earlier to shape the collective memory of the Okie exodus. The construction of this memory continues in the nation's historical consciousness, to which the Babb sisters' neglected legacy will doubtlessly contribute. The Dust Bowl migration was an epochal event defining in part what is characteristically American: the ecological destruction of a region, the irreversible rupture of traditional farming cultures and economies, and ultimately the reintegration of a dispossessed people into new communities and modes of living. In this great transformation Sanora discovered subjects for her writing. Through time this signal event in American history entered the national consciousness as a memory site, symbolizing the perils of failure in a capitalist economy and the inevitable social transformations.

A number of notable historical studies have attempted to supplement and correct the large corpus of individual memories, political discourse, and creative interpretations of the events. These have contributed to the creation of the Dust Bowl (a journalist invented the term) as cultural memory whose surface of stark images masks a complex subject that bears on events today. A farm family carrying their worldly belongings along a highway, flivvers with bald tires and mattresses lashed to the roof, fence posts buried in dust, the care-lined faces of migrant mothers: these are part of a larger collective memory, inspiring literary and film production and altering the way in which people respond to economic downturns. In people's minds are images of dispossession shaped by the cultural memory of the 1930s, as if a specter of dispossession looms over society, haunting our deepest fears and warning us to be prepared for the next Depression.

2 FIELD NOTES

. . . the disease of uprootedness . . . has been inflicted on the working class.

SIMONE WEIL

In spring 1934 Sanora traveled from Los Angeles to visit her mother, Jennie Parks Babb, in Garden City, Kansas, where she had apprenticed as a journalist on the *Garden City Telegram.* For many of the literary radicals of the 1930s journalism was preparation for literary work, as it had been for Stephen Crane, Theodore Dreiser, Ernest Hemingway, Sherwood Anderson, Katherine Anne Porter, Martha Gellhorn, Willa Cather, Edna Ferber, Zona Gale, and others. The Depression era needed writers who were able to record its tumultuous events and tragic human exigencies.

A terrible drought afflicted the High Plains in 1934. For fifty-eight days that summer the temperature exceeded 100 degrees; rainfall was less than half of normal. Little fodder other than Russian thistle grew to feed starving cattle. During Sanora's visit, a "black blizzard" of dust turned noon dark. Traffic stopped, businesses closed; in vain people used sheets to cover windows and stuffed newspapers into cracks. The wind raged ceaselessly for a day, blowing dust through the cracks and choking livestock. The dust destroyed auto engines and caused respiratory illnesses that people referred to as "dust pneumonia." Finney County's funds were soon exhausted. Relief rolls soared, schools closed, farms were abandoned or foreclosed. Two years later the dust storms returned, along with a plague of grasshoppers infesting most of the western plains states.

The New Deal provided programs of relief and employment. The Agricultural Adjustment Act of 1933 made payments to bolster wheat prices and remove land from cultivation. The Works Projects Administration employed men in the construction of roads and sanitation facilities. When in early 1936 the Supreme Court declared the AAA unconstitutional, local communities were obliged to pick up the burden of providing for the poor. To receive relief payments for groceries and rent, men performed public works projects such as digging ditches on

Dust storm over highway near Dalhart, Texas, by Arthur Rothstein, FSA, LC-USF34-2485-D

Garden City's Main Street. Dust storms blew up again, but news of gas wells discovered nearby boosted spirits.

During her trip to Kansas in 1934, Sanora made a brief visit to Forgan in the Oklahoma Panhandle, where ten years earlier she had graduated from high school. In an unpublished manuscript, "Oklahoma Panhandle, 1934," she recorded her impressions of the toll of economic hardship and drought on the lives of the dusted out farmers and once prosperous townspeople. In it she details the economic ravages of crop failures and "drouth"—a colloquialism particular to the Southwest—that foreshadow dispossession and exodus. The class differences that she had suffered as a gambler's daughter, Sanora wryly observed, were temporarily effaced by a failing economy.

The town she had known during the relative prosperity of World War I, when there was strong demand for agricultural produce, was now a distressed community where residents faced an uncertain future. Sanora hoped that a new political consciousness would spring from the growing awareness that simply waiting for better times was no longer an option. Her own political consciousness found expression in reportage, short stories, and activism, including work with the Farm Security Administration through which she met and aided the same plains

Farm buildings half buried in sand, by Dorothea Lange, FSA, LC-05262-131557

people who, in taking flight, as she predicted they would, made their desperate choice.

Oklahoma Panhandle, 1934:

In this little town in Oklahoma with its broken walks and dirt streets and its two or three hundred people and its farmers living on the prairies around it, I saw them standing in line for the meat and potatoes of relief. I saw the people I used to know who had lived smugly in their imaginary stratas—the *best* people who had bathtubs and cars, the middle ones who had bathtubs and white collar jobs, the unacceptable ones who had no bathtubs, manual jobs or doubtful means of support—standing in line together. The essential differences in these people in the first place had been very slight, and now with the superficial gloss gone, and hunger a near and known thing to all of them, their stricken faces, one after another in the line, looked very much alike. The men had always had more ease together than the women but now they with their skins uncreamed and no place for their snobberies, they stood together forgetting their old ways.

This is just one little town but I thought of all the other towns I had known and not known in the sections of Texas, New Mexico, Colorado and Kansas that seam this strip of Oklahoma, and all the towns everywhere with their people gathering into the tight knots of distress and painful wonder at this unending process of decay that levels their lives down to a single want and fear. Here it was a warm winter day with wind that smelled of spring when people stir in their selves for a new season and think of work and change. And what would there be of change for them but the deadness of time without work and the waiting for food relief days? The little main street was quiet; two old Ford touring cars were parked in the middle of the street. No one came in and out of the stores. Four of the town's college graduates were sitting in the drugstore window. There wasn't any life anywhere. From each end of the main street I could look out onto the drouth-desolated fields where no new crops were planted or would be planted this spring, not only because of the drouth. The farmers know that they can't afford now to plant a crop or, if there were rain, to care for it until the doubtful selling stage. They cannot get anything so complicated through their heads as the benefit of having plowed under and limited crop production when the need is greater than they have ever known.

Another day I inquired about a teacher I had liked, and since the schools were closed for lack of funds, I found that she was living on a poor little farm several miles from the town. When I got there she was closed away in a middle room with three grandchildren and two children from a nearby farm. She was teaching the children from old school books she had saved, each child being in a different class. One of them was in the eighth grade, and this would doubtless be her last year in school. The windows were closed against the sand blowing outside and the air was dry and thick and hard to breathe. She wasn't complaining that she was out of a job; she had taught too long to stop with the end of one. She *was* concerned over the future of these children, and hundreds like them in other places where schools were closed or only open a few months in the year.

Without a depression this country is hard and bitter to live in, whipped with high winds and dust storms, baked in the summers with a dry electric air, and with winters that are cold and sometimes snowless. The people have had to fight for their hard living in the *good* times before the exploitation sore came to a head, as well as in the lean times. They speak of getting one good crop year out of four, enough in the meantime to get them through until the big year. There may not be enough snow in the winter to bed the fall crops waiting in the ground. Before the seeds have rooted themselves in the autumn or spring, the windstorms may blow the seed out, transferring the soil halfway across the state or even into another one. There may not be enough rain in the summer to keep the crop growing; in that case, it burns, dry hot winds that burn a crop in a few days. The crop may get to the harvesting stage and be hailed out. This is the worst dread of all. There are frequent electric storms and the farmers watch the clouds and sniff the air for signs of hail every time dark clouds gather. A rarer danger, although I have seen it happen several times, is the burning of ripe crops fired by lightning. There is always the need among the farmers, save the *boss* farmers owning thousands of acres, to sell after harvest when the price is usually low. Few of them can afford to store their crops and wait for the price to go up.

You might wonder that they stay in such a place at all. It is as if they knew no other and wanted none: it is home. The prosperous used to drive to California in the summers but few of them moved. Many of the retired moved away from the Midwest, but few of the workers, and in this region few of them ever have a chance to retire. They are willing to struggle with the natural difficulties, and for a long time they were willing enough to face the new ones coming from (to them) an unknown source. But they are beginning to wonder now, there have been other drouths, it has always been hard to make a living, but there is something now they cannot get their hands on. "It don't seem right," they say, "when a man can't work for his livin'." Their cars are gone, their stock, their houses, their land, their money, their work, and they come into the town or out of its houses and fall in line for the meat and potatoes of relief. They don't want to keep on living by relief, and if no one else has been able to change this condition in the years since 1929, they have begun to think that perhaps it is up to them. They had been taking government for granted; they thought it was theirs; they thought America somehow belonged to the people and America was to them this strip of Oklahoma where they have worked all their lives, and it had belonged to them until now. I heard their questions and groping faltering answers, and I heard them say over and over again they must *stick together* now. But they do not quite know how to unite and make it known: they are ready and they need to know, and someone must make it clear to them that there is a way. Otherwise they will go on in a stricken, prideless way believing themselves forgotten in these small dark places. Some of them are "educated" and wondering, many of them are ignorant and backward, because they have been too poor to benefit by our *free* opportunities, but they are all hungry. The old false bourgeois prides are gone; they are waiting mindlessly for some new pride to take its place. There is only one thing that will give it to them—the sense of necessity to come together as a mass. They know the necessity; someone must tell them what is to be done and how they can move out of their animal despair into hope.

These little communities that spot the plains are for the most part unaware of the knowledge that has penetrated the cities and busier agricultural districts where workers have learned to unite with some hope.

They produce such a small share of the goods that living to them has only an immediate significance. They do not often know of much that goes on outside their narrow boundaries, and their own restless questioning too frequently meets the "superior" opinion of one or two men in the town or county giving off Chamber of Commerce slogans with a vengeance that makes them think any progressive ideas that may have leaked in are the wildest heresy. But these slogans that worked miracles in their ears once are getting a little too familiar to have any effect.

In some of the towns where there is still the pretense left in the petty strivings of the "upper" class, I heard the scorn and the doubt of unity, the ignorance and the fear of change, but here in these wasted places this empty emotion is gone long ago. There were never any classes but the lower-middle and lower, but the distinctions were sharp into imagined upper, middle and lower. The property snobbery was strong and evil. These class divisions have been almost dissolved by the crisis, by loss of almost the only barrier, property, and by hunger and despair. You cannot put the cherished "culture and refinement" into any one of these classes; almost the only difference is the slight and often false and unenlightened veneer acquired at the state universities. The only persons I know who have pulled themselves out of the backwardness of the place to any fuller development of their capacities and point of view are from the snubbed lower class. The town and the county fall in line for the meat and potatoes of relief—the unity of despair they now feel is only a short step away from the unity of action. They need and are ready for someone to show them the way—the way out to the right to work and live in America as the free people they have been deluded into thinking they were. They have nothing to look forward to this year and the next but relief. In the blind groping, some of them talk of migrating to other states, thinking to escape the drouth area they may escape depression. Where will they go in America to escape?

"Triple A, Dusted Out"

Low market prices of cotton and wheat induced desperate landowners to sign up for AAA payments. Reduced land under tillage meant less need for sharecroppers, who comprised the majority of farmers in the South, as well as Oklahoma and Texas. By 1940, James N. Gregory notes, farm tenancy was down by 24 percent: "The era of tenant farming in the Southwest was drawing to a close" (13). Similarly, efforts to cut hog production met with unintentional consequences, as Babb records in her journal in early spring 1938.

Note on the government's AAA program to reduce hog production and corn acreage:
Mr. K had a litter of pigs [that were] over the allotted amount. Forbidden to feed them, to sell them or give them away—[he was] supposed to sell them. Joe hadn't enough. He wanted to buy. [Mr. K] couldn't sell or give them but he would leave them there and Joe could come by and steal them. He did.

An allotment paid the farmer for a fixed percentage of land to be left uncultivated, according to a formula based on the land's recorded productivity over a given period. Some farmers had not kept their grain elevator receipts; as a result allotments often were inaccurate, penalizing the farmer. Sanora notes:

Joe planted winter wheat in September. When it was up he rec'd a letter saying he wouldn't receive his money because he had broken his contract. Confused, [he was] afraid to plant anything.

The Dispossessed

Evictions, foreclosures, failed crops, bankruptcy, drought left hundreds of thousands of dispossessed farmers without assistance, overburdening an emergency relief system that supported more than half the population of eastern Oklahoma. The dispossessed flooded makeshift squatter encampments along riverbanks and near stockyards, joining the unemployed from towns and cities, many of whom had held white-collar jobs. The ensuing stream of refugees heading west in search of work comprised a diverse mix of professionals, skilled and un-

LEFT: *"Bindlestiff"—itinerant worker*

RIGHT: *Southern Pacific Railroad billboard*

Tom Collins and Sanora Babb

skilled workers, clerks, farmers, farm laborers, and failed businessmen. Swelling the stream were independent farmers from the High Plains, dusted out by prolonged droughts. These were Sanora's own people. They came as families together however they could—walking, hitchhiking, crowded into overloaded, worn vehicles—lured by the prospect of work.

In California the refugees encountered a system of peonage dating from Spanish California, the colonial character of which continued into statehood as a result of the feudalistic Mexican land grants. "The ownership," McWilliams argues in his landmark study, *Factories in the Field*, "changed from Mexican grantee to American capitalist; the grant, as such, remained" (15). Racial segregation was familiar to refugees from the South, but few had experienced divisions along ethnic lines.

As assistant to FSA administrator Tom Collins Sanora registered the refugees seeking a temporary home and health care in the government camps, organized committees of refugees to run the camps, and wrote reports describing their needs and conditions. Over a period of nearly a year, Collins and Babb worked their way north from the Imperial Valley into the San Joaquin and Sacramento Valleys and farther north to Oregon. They helped to set up camps, installed managers, and walked the roads encouraging refugees in their makeshift shelters to seek the better conditions of the government camps. Babb and Collins were constantly on the move until they reached the San Joaquin Valley in spring 1938, permitting Sanora little time to make more than brief notes, which she recorded in a 5-by-7-inch leather-bound journal. In the following note Babb recorded how Anglo refugees were made aware that "whiteness" set them apart from other categories of ethnic groups.

Labor Conditions:
First "Orientals" were brought in for building railroads, mostly Chinese and Japanese. Mexicans gradually were brought in and displaced Oriental farm labor. [Then] Filipinos. Dust Bowl refugees gradually [are] replacing all other farm labor, although Mexicans and Filipinos still have high numbers. This influx of "white" labor raises the social status of the farm worker; the native Californian has always shunned work, hiring other races to do it. This raising of the social status however is merely a superficial one, of seeing a "white" do the work formerly associated with other races. The "white" migrant lives in the same poor conditions that the Mexican and Filipino are forced into, but there is more interest in raising their standards, simply in defense, because they fear a majority of children growing up will be of the migratory farm labor class.

"By the end of the decade [1920s]," McWilliams wrote, "the industrial character of California agriculture was firmly established. The industry was organized from top to bottom; methods of operation had been thoroughly rationalized; control tended more and more to be vested in the hands of the large growers; and the dominance of finance was greater than ever."[1] The methods of industry applied to agriculture were changing the nature of farming, Sanora noted. A new "Farmer-Industrialist" would eventually force out the independent farmer. Commenting on an advertisement by a San Francisco bank that read "[The] application of industrial methods to farming during the last generation has made California the leading agricultural state of the nation," Sanora wrote:

Farmer-Industrialist:
Specialization. Product Research. Mass Production. Co-Operative Marketing. Asparagus, prunes, walnuts, lettuce, vineyards, orchards. . . . Crops produced annually in excess of $600,000,000. Banks helped to industrialize agriculture. The small independent farmer [is] almost extinct.

From 1901 to 1929 the AFL had made many attempts, all unsuccessful, to organize farm and cannery workers.[2] It showed little interest in organizing itinerant agricultural workers. "Only fanatics," an AFL spokesperson in California remarked, "are willing to live in shacks or tents and get their heads broken in the interests of migratory labor."[3] The Depression witnessed radical changes in labor organization, including the founding of the CIO in 1936. In the Imperial Valley in 1930 Mexican and Filipino fruit and vegetable harvesters along with Anglo cannery workers struck in reaction to wage cuts. Trade Union Unity League organizers quickly moved in, enlisting workers, and when the strike failed, they conferred a meeting of the workers.

Invoking the Criminal Syndicalism Act, the government arrested the organizers, sending seven to San Quentin prison. By the following year, the Communist Party had made dramatic gains in organizing farmworkers and cannery workers in the Cannery and Agricultural Workers' Industrial Union. Perhaps the earliest successful attempt to organize migrant workers in California's fields in the 1930s, it precipitated violent reaction. Deputized vigilantes, small-town police, and employer-paid thugs used strong-arm methods to intimidate the hapless field workers. Confrontations peaked in 1933 and 1934 in a series of bitterly fought strikes in California's Central Valley that served to consolidate the CAWIU and embolden Party organizers despite a hostile press, police violence, retributive courts, and, in several instances, National Guard troops.

The climax of this early labor protest occurred on July 20, 1934, in the arrest of some eighteen CAWIU leaders. "Raiding parties," McWilliams notes, "armed with sawed-off shotguns, handcuffs, blackjacks, rubber hose, billies, riot clubs, gas bombs and accompanied by news reporters and photographers from the *Sacramento Bee,* raided the Workers' Center in Sacramento, and arrested the leaders of the CAWIU, including Caroline Decker and Pat Chambers."[4] The strikes netted wage increases but collapsed the CAWIU and stiffened resistance by a loose but powerful group of large landowners, financial institutions, farm corporations, and right-wing legislators. These found common cause through the newly formed Associated Farmers of California, Inc.

Working in informal alliance with local police, the Associated Farmers deputized members, planted spies among labor groups, and sponsored antipicketing ordinances as "emergency-disaster" measures. Their activities amounted in some cases to pure terrorism as they attempted to quell strikes and break the resolve of labor organizers.

In the relatively brief period following the collapse of the CAWIU and before the arrival en masse of Anglo refugees from the midland and southern states, the most militant labor protest occurred among Filipinos and Mexican laborers. They had little legal protection against arrest and repression; moreover, they were increasingly displaced (and deported) as desperate Anglo refugees, most of whom lacked experience in labor organization, replaced them in the fields.[5]

Organized labor found an ally among Democrats under the New Deal; by the mid-1930s the CIO had supplanted the conservative AFL as an effective force in promulgating workers' rights. California was deeply divided following the 1934 governor's race, in which Upton Sinclair's End Poverty in California Party pulled some four hundred thousand Democrats away, splitting the party's vote and assuring the reelection of Republican Governor Frank Merriam.

The arrival of the Dust Bowl refugees threatened to burden California's relief costs while raising expectations that they would support left political candidates who proposed increased social services. Radical activists and liberals rallied to the side of the refugees. Some worked as volunteers, giving medical aid and collecting clothing and joining groups such as the Simon Lubin Society and the Steinbeck Committee to Aid Agricultural Organization. A larger commitment was required of activists who joined as labor organizers and served with the Farm Security Administration in the fields.

Not blind to the opportunity, CIO organizers signed up refugee workers in anticipation of the 1938 election. Again efforts to organize the workers were met with powerful resistance, through an organization formed in 1938 called the California Citizens Association (CCA), whose purpose was to deal with the state's "migrant problem."[6] The CCA targeted federal relief agencies, especially the Works Progress Administration and granting programs offered by the FSA. The CCA, portraying the refugees as welfare freeloaders, found support in *Los Angeles Times* editorials and publications of the American Legion, the Associated Farmers, and local chambers of commerce.

The election of a Democrat, Culbert Olson, to the governorship in

LEFT: *Strike committee with organizer*

RIGHT: *Strike committee, organizers*

1938 boosted the workers' efforts to obtain a fair wage and decent working conditions. Yet the argument that Olson's generous relief policies encouraged more migrants to seek work in California, further burdening taxpayers, continued to gain support. The issue divided California's legislature, which eventually dismantled the State Emergency Relief Administration and assigned responsibility for relief to local counties. In 1941, however, the Supreme Court overruled attempts to enforce the state's Indigent Act criminalizing the transport of indigent persons into California.

Neither side solved the "migrant problem," nor did the demand for seasonal labor end with World War II. War industries absorbed the Dust

Picket car

Picket captain, Shafter strike

LEFT: *Picket line, Shafter, with front sign reading, "Come to our mass meeting"*

RIGHT: *Picket line, Shafter, with signs reading, "Be fair and join us" and "Don't scab"*

Bowl workers, creating the need to again import field workers from Mexico. In August 1939 Sanora noted the obstacles facing the various labor groups, including rivalries, the inclusion of ethnic groups, and company unionism, for instance, the charge against Edward Vandeleur, State Federation of Labor secretary, that he and the AFL permitted company-friendly union organization in the cannery industry. Sanora wrote in her journal:

Organization of labor:
[The] CIO is consolidating its forces everywhere to get through the more intensive unemployment period. . . . [A]griculture and workers are demanding to be organized.

Vandeleur's phony AFL unions in the canneries [are] being investigated now by the NLRB [National Labor Relations Board]. Charges filed by the CIO. The whole cannery setup of company unions (closed shop) is such a stinking mess from beginning to end you can be sure the NLRB will do a thorough job in order to take the whole thing into court as a hole-proof case.

The chief trouble before was that the cannery, agriculture, and packing unions have always been split. That is what happened at the bloody Salinas lettuce strike in 1936. The failure of the unity of racial groups [underscores] the necessity of unity with Filipinos and Mexicans and all other racial minority groups.

WPA wage rate for Tulare County [is] the lowest in the state.

New problems facing workers in cotton planting this year. [The] invention and manufacture of cotton chopper which hoe, chop, etc., cotton, thus taking the place of thousands of men and women.

Government Camps

In the course of setting up FSA tent camps for the refugees and registering the workers, Sanora reported on social and health conditions among refugees, for instance, the mounting hostility on the part of small-town residents (taxpayers) in the Central Valley, school officials, and vigilantes. When the initial vanguard of immigrant Anglos turned into a flood of desperate refugees, Californians came to view them as a debased, barely human folk, ignorant, uncouth, and unwelcome. Local newspapers and the conservative *Los Angeles Times* played up the social burdens that the Dust Bowl refugees imposed on the state. California taxpayers came to see them as an invading host straining local coffers. Small-town residents, noting the rise in criminal behavior, attributed it to the Okies or their influence. The reaction to the refugee workers, ranging from cruel negligence to violence, added only to their misery. To Sanora these reactions were evidence of

Fascist characteristics of the campaign against the migratory workers in California:
—Concerted objections of women to children of the scorned "Okies" attending public schools. (Okie: anybody who lives in a tent or shack—an insult used against the children at school as well as the grownups.) The agitation and pressure of the various reactionary organizations resulting in the government building one school in Kern County especially for the migrants. Note: Agitation of big growers, chamber of commerce men, etc., for a change in the school law which makes it compulsory for children to attend school up to the age of 18. They want it changed to 8th grade limit. One of them said, "Why, if all people send their kids to school until they are 18, we'll never have any farm laborers, and wages will go up besides."
—This stigmatization now felt by children can only result in one attitude in later life: Jim-Crowism for the worker.
—Children here are in persistent struggle, that can not be let up for a moment, to attend public school—in rags but clean. They are picked up by school buses, or are taken part way by their parents, or they walk. This public school attendance has a very significant and natural way of helping the conditions of these workers. Quite naturally they suffer the stig-

matism of being an "Okie" at school, among the "respectable" people. Naturally they come home and question their mothers as to why they are different, why they wear rags when the others do not, why they are hungry and the others well fed, etc.? The mothers react by "getting after" the father to change this; the father begins to fight for organization and better pay and better living conditions.

—Parties: another method of mingling the children. While the parents of the "normal" children despise the presence of the Okies in their fair land, and try to keep their children separated, it is true that even though children taunt them for being Okies and for their rags, they are more naturally friendly. Sometimes a camp manager takes a few dollars of his own money and gives a little party for the children, to which they invite their schoolmates. The children attend, have a good time, but go home with tales of the camp and the strange way they live. In this way many parents have been brought to sympathy. Sometimes they are invited to a return party, and this has its effect when the mothers are suddenly astounded to recognize other differences in the children besides rags: the Okies are sharper, more resourceful, more able to take care of themselves, think for themselves. Maybe they are after all worth helping?

I have heard it repeatedly said that California could become a fascist state tomorrow, so well organized is it with vigilantes, reactionaries, etc. This is the seat of high finance, agriculture, gun-guarded, violence-encircled. The great sun valleys of California are infested with hired forces and hired spying—to keep organization of labor down, to keep wages low, to keep people in need so that they are willing to pick the fruit and the cotton,

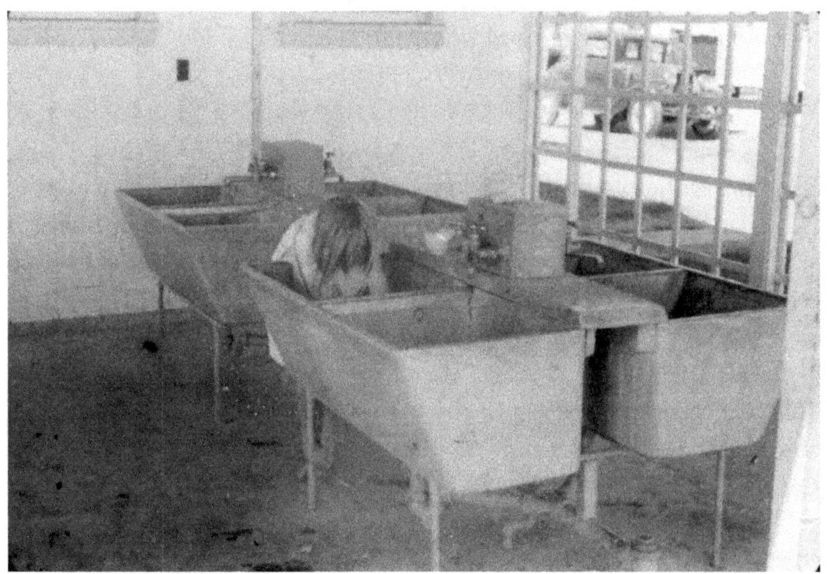

Girl washing clothes in FSA camp washhouse

FSA *clinic, Shafter*

plant and harvest the vegetables for whatever low wage they are offered. Their [landowners'] greed obscures their vision. Their industrial myopia does not let them see how much they stimulate the very thing they fight. Or, if they see it, they believe in the might of their power to beat and choke the impulse of every man and woman to live a decent life.

Babb began her work with the FSA near Brawley and El Centro in the Imperial Valley. By late February, as the harvesting moved northward, she arrived in Tulare County, in California's Central Valley, where she recorded these observations in her journal:

Visalia 2/24/38:
This year 250,000 acres less of cotton to be planted here, and that means about 60,000 people wandering around starving. (Act just passed by Congress for crop control.)

Wahoo: weed that grows in semi-arid lands, used for medicine, to doctor almost everything.

Oklahomans, referred to as "Okies," are held in derision.

January-February-March, the migratory workers are at their lowest ebb. There is no work during these months, and it isn't likely they could save anything on the few months work.
August-September, the migrants make the most money. Fruit [is] ripe then.

600 million dollars was the annual farm income for 1937. 57% of all people gainfully employed in agriculture are farm laborers.

As soon as work is over, [company] camps on ranches are torn down and workers driven off.

Migrant tent—woman in bed, too hungry and weak to get up. Children sitting around hungry and weak. The man walking down the road to find something to do, or something to eat, fainted from hunger, and can't go on.

FSA *clinic, Shafter*

Deserted milk house: starving mother and father and six children, all with the measles but none of them in bed.

Problem of getting the mattress off the floor. Relief man suggests the dump, and they go there and find an old bed.

RM: (to migrant farmer): "Well, wouldn't you rather have that 800 acre farm back there in Oklahoma than this?"
MF: "No sir, I'd rather be here like this. I ain't never goin' back there. I couldn't raise nothin', do nothin'. Why I couldn't even have a good time on that 800 acres if I had a keg of whiskey."
Cotton—
Wages: 75 cents to $1 per cwt. depending upon the labor supply.

Labor contractor—
[A] labor parasite who makes a double profit on wages, and one or other of his various schemes.

Labor contractor drives thru the country, stopping at farms, makes estimates of amount of cotton, and makes an offer to the grower to pick it for so much.

Then he drives along the camps, talks to the "Okies" and tells them all to go to a certain farm where several hundred men are needed, at good wages (perhaps at 80 cents), etc. Then he drives to another camp and repeats the offer, and more men go to these farms. Finally where 300 men are actually needed 1,000, or 2,500 men will appear. The offered price at once comes down, and most of them leave without work. They have arrived with their last bit of gas and no food at "home" so that they are forced to take anything.

Aside from the wage profiteering, the l.c. [labor contractor] has several systems by which he derives another bit from the temporary wages of these poverty stricken people.

(1) The l.c. goes to the grocer, tells him that he has so many men contracted, and is going to pay them in scrip. He will send all the men there to cash their scrip and buy their groceries, if the grocer will give him a cut. On the surface that is quite legal: the scrip is good as money, it can be cashed at the grocer's. It is an obvious point to mention, that the men seldom have any cash to them.

(2) The cotton pickers bring in their sacks to be weighed. Of course, the weigh man is a stooge of the contractor, as is the "worker" who has started a dice game there. The l.c. owns the dice game too. Workers who

have just received their pay are urged to "get in and win a little." Those who play lose their wages, or whatever part they risked.

The small farmer is somewhat sympathetic to the farm laborer because he is learning that he is nothing more than a "glorified" farm laborer himself. He borrows from the finance company to plant his crop, and the crop returns go to the company. Maybe he gets a little cash left over; maybe he gets in debt to the company. The small farmer is almost extinct in the great farm valleys of California, which are controlled by high finance—big growers, absentee owners. One of the big owners is the United Fruit Company.

Remark made by a State official, also local c of c [chamber of commerce] man: "You know what ought to be done with these people? We ought to damn all the rivers in the state and drive them into them."

E. Clemens Horst, one of the largest hop ranchers in the west (Oregon). He is not a member of the Associated Farmers. . . . "I've never joined a farmer group because I don't have their ideas. Something happens and they want to call out the police dept., the army, the navy, and sometimes the fire dept. Then they begin buying tear gas, and start fashioning clubs. . . ."

Average [income] for a family is around $300 a year.

Walter Cowan, vice president of the State Federation of Labor: "Every attempt so far by the workers to raise their living conditions to the level somewhere in keeping with our American standard of living has been met with a vicious onslaught of tear gas, shooting and beatings inspired by the Associated Farmers."

Kinds of camps in California:

1. U.S. Govt. camp—or "demonstrational" camps. Seven in California.

2. Grower camps. Operated on property of grower, with growers' consent. Grower either gives free tent space or charges rent. Furnishes water and the poorest kind of toilet.

3. Squatter camps (66 here, about 2,000 in the state)—Any group of tents or makeshift shacks on private property, without consent of owner and absolutely barren of any sanitary facilities. Usually on absentee owner land. (United Fruit Company owns thousands of acres in the state, and is one of the most reactionary.)

Birthrate:

About the only way to touch the interest of the thousands of women who are continually asking that migratory workers' children not be permitted to attend public schools along with their children, that the men and women be sterilized because they are poor, that they be driven out, and so on, is that cold, astounding presentation of facts about the birthrate. Our national average birthrate is three, which is, of course, a rather high figure. The average birthrate per family of the people sub-marginal incomes is between 4.5 and 5. This means that the birthrate among those who can well afford birth control is very low. The large families of the poor, sometimes counting up to 14 and 15, will grow up out of their starvation and their oppression with their memories of being arrested, beaten, kicked about, stigmatized, driven from place to place. And they will far overshadow the offspring of the upper bracket incomes—the children who have been raised in health and care and protection.

The spectre of the future is not a pleasant one for the comfortable and secure to consider. There are two ways out of this: (a) to secure the complete suppression and oppression of the people with fascism; (b) to help them—not with charity, not with their sterilized sympathies, but with active aid for change in their immediate living conditions when the simple right to work will be restored.

Being among these families, seeing the appalling conditions which they survive, the spectacle is not pleasant for anyone, *but for other reasons*. The mothers and fathers are starved, the children are starved. It seems every mother is pregnant, or trying to nurse a baby at a dry breast, or has just suffered a miscarriage. This last is even more devastating to the precarious health of the mothers than childbirth, but many of them are in such malnourished conditions they cannot carry their children to birth. It is all the more amazing that many of them do. Childbirth is a terrible thing for a woman suffering and emaciated with starvation. But these women endure the heightened labor pains, the agonies of birth without a doctor, without medical care of any kind save the few simple things the camp manager has perhaps been able to teach them. The camp manager himself, a relief official, may have to help bring the child into the world. One of them has lost count of the number he has delivered in his years of work.

Only a few days ago we met a young man walking along the road to town in search of immediate work and help. His wife had had a baby three days before in an abandoned milk house separated from any camp, where they had taken refuge during the recent storms. He was desperate. Since the birth, his wife, their other children and he himself had not eaten for three days. If he did not get something for them at once, she and the baby would die.

You, who live in any kind of comfort or convenience, do not know how these people can survive these things, do you? How can a modern woman have a baby without a doctor? How could she then be without food for three days, without any kind of care, or the usual sanitary and sterilized attention? How can she nurse her baby at a dry breast, and what will she do when there is not other food for the baby, and the baby cries incessantly from hunger? How can she keep her sanity when everyday she sees her children getting big eyes and swollen bellies? What does she think when she goes to bed one night and is too weak to get up the next morning?

Well, she is a woman such as you will never be because you live differently. She has developed resourcefulness—courage and endurance that we never know we have. Her husband and her children have developed it too.

They will make something to eat if there is *anything* growing. They will endure because there is no immediate escape from endurance. They will find medicine growing on the earth where they live. There is a weed called wahoo—you brew it and drink it for everything, and it helps.

But, of course, there's a limit to starvation, a limit to pain, a limit to endurance, patience, struggle. Some will die. *The rest must live.*

In answer to the frequent threat to the farmers: "What right have they to come into California and *demand any*thing! They ought to be glad we don't drive them out."

"We thought that America was a free country and we could move wherever we want to, but it don't seem like it here. If we harvest their crops, why haven't we the right to demand honest pay for honest work. They won't find us complainin' at fair treatment."

California has always extended an invitation to farm labor, providing the labor is cheap, and unorganized. Labor surplus was always a desired and welcome weapon against wage struggles.

A Justice of Peace said, after having a talk about migrants, "I never realized these people are humans."

Incident of farmer sending children $1^1/2$ miles for new shoes. . . . [The] Mother said [to Tom Collins], who had come in for a call, muddy and wet, [that] she had bought shoes for her son who was to be the bridegroom, with the last of the relief check, because she wanted him to be married in decent shoes.

Memo of camps: newfound freedom of women expressed particularly in saving money for insurance, savings, etc. First week [the] husbands were urged to show their checks to [their] wives (something they had never done before), and give them so much for household expenses.

Soon the women began to show Tom [Collins] the money they had saved. They were carrying it in their stockings, bosoms, and inside hatbands of husbands' old discarded hats they wore.

In the fields, 1938:
493 home visits, 2,512 people seen in homes. 242 [homes] signed up personally representing 1,312, [thus total of] 3,825.

The real opposition [to government camps] comes from a few big farmers who are fearful such camps eventually will germinate labor troubles.

Large Landowners

Wages and housing, Sanora observed, varied among the big growers. Several, like Hubert C. Merritt, in exchange for lower wages furnished tiny cabins to the labor migrants at $4 a month. Workers at the 7,000-acre Tagus Ranch at Tulare, in the Central Valley, chose between FSA tent camps when they were available or rented one-room shacks. One of the better camps, owned by Allan Hoover, was located at Greenfield in Kern County, where alfalfa and cotton were grown. Hoover also managed the 3,200-acre Sierra Vista Ranch at Coachella and a 1,800-acre ranch of vineyards and vegetables at Wasco. Word quickly got around that refugees should be wary of the Frick Ranch, owned by the Kern County Land Company, as well as H. H. Hare's cotton farm, which employed mainly blacks in execrable physical conditions. Elmer Houchin, once a poor man but now "reputedly the richest man in Kern County," Babb

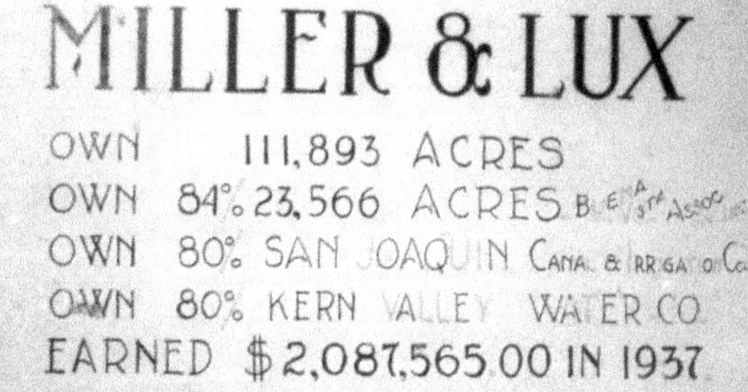

ABOVE LEFT:
Billboard of the Miller & Lux corporate farm near Merced, California

ABOVE RIGHT:
Miller & Lux sign detailing the corporate farm's assets

Sheep farm owned by Miller & Lux

noted, ran one of the worst privately owned camps for migrant workers. His hobby was breeding exotic peacocks and pheasants. Houchin owned 52,000 acres in Kern County, headed twenty-one businesses, managed Miller & Lux, one of the early California corporate farms, and was the General Motors distributor for the county.

If, as studies show, the rich spend relatively little money in proportion to their wealth, Houchin saved a great deal. Despite a law requiring water for domestic purposes at the camps, Houchin's workers had to walk five miles to fetch potable water, hauling it back in pails. "It is not easy," Sanora observed, "to keep clean under these conditions."

On a qualitative scale of labor relations Allan Hoover ranked far above Elmer Houchin. Someplace in between was Joseph Di Giorgio, who had large landholdings near Bakersfield. Perhaps the largest individual producer of citrus in the United States at that time, Di Giorgio owned orchards in Washington, Idaho, and Florida. Together these growers possessed immense political and economic power. When newspaper articles in San Francisco criticized them, they threatened a food boycott of the city.

Sunkist
Oranges
Lemons

TAGUS RANCH

TAGUS RANCH

Billboard—to discourage workers from striking

OPPOSITE PAGE

TOP LEFT: *Sunkist packing plant, Murphy Ranch*

TOP RIGHT: *Grain elevator, Von Glahn Corporation*

ABOVE LEFT: *Sunkist Packing Company sheds*

ABOVE RIGHT: *Company-owned shacks for migrant workers*

BELOW LEFT: *Home of a corporate farmer*

BELOW RIGHT: *Calpak peaches en route to Del Monte Packing*

BOTTOM LEFT: *Tagus Ranch, Visalia. H. C. Merritt & Son, owner, 7,000 acres. "World's largest peach, apricot and nectarine orchard"*

BOTTOM RIGHT: *Café and ranch offices, Tagus Ranch, Visalia*

Antiunion efforts, orchestrated by important landowners through their influence in the California legislature, succeeded in collapsing the Cannery and Agricultural Workers Industrial Union in 1934, following a series of angry, violent strikes in the San Joaquin and Imperial Valleys.[7] Led mainly by Communist Party organizers, the strikes were ultimately crushed by the National Guard, police, and "company goons." Their organizational efforts broken, the workers, Filipinos, Mexicans, and Anglos, nonetheless engaged in a dramatic struggle that set the stage for union activism that was soon to follow.

What was needed was a union offering national representation for migratory workers who in the course of their work crossed state borders. This representation finally came through the United Cannery, Agricultural, Packing and Allied Workers of America, established after a meeting in Denver, Colorado, in 1937 (McWilliams 272).

The resurgence of labor organization heightened the conflict between workers and farm owners. The latter, together with the canneries and shippers, had tight control of the entire farm industry, fixing prices, holding wage levels down, and so forth, through the California Fruit Growers Exchange, which was in effect, as McWilliams noted, a "huge holding corporation" (279–280). Moreover, most Anglo refugees had little experience with union activity. Their education and backgrounds differed greatly: the independent farmers on the High Plains had little in common with sharecroppers from Arkansas and eastern Oklahoma, who were used to a paternalistic system of landownership and tenancy. Former tradespeople from small towns in the Midwest felt shame about being viewed as common field workers. The refugees' pride was hurt, but as Sanora remarked often, they held fast to their tattered dignity.

There were risks in confronting their employers, who, with the growing surplus of labor, would dismiss a worker for attending a union meeting. Dismissal meant losing one's shelter and having to move on to find work elsewhere. In some cases, when there was no place for the refugees to go and no money to get there, growers provided space for improvised shelter, which, in the following journal note, was called "Rag Town."

Rag Town
—Cotton pickers' strike
—Picket line by field
—Some /workers/ wish "they would go away so I can work."
—Arrest all.
—Family in cabin, company owned. Know they will be put out if strike. Sympathetic with strike, as all are save the stools [informers], but decide to and are told to get out at once. Refuse [to leave until they receive] three days' notice. . . . Finally law sets all things in road and drives car out. Put sick man out on road too.
—No place to go—so company permits space. Set up Rag Town.
—Man mortgaging trailer for $50 for strike. Another gives $16.
—Some injuries, jail, but strike goes on.

Refugee Needs

Heavy rains flooded camps in the San Joaquin Valley in early 1938 and throughout the spring. Sanora noted in her journal:

It's rainy and suddenly very cold. The tent floors are all wet, and most of the bed covers damp. With nothing to do, and a need to forget hunger, they go to bed very early. . . . [T]he rains cut out whole season of work, adding two more months to unemployment of farm workers. Annual incomes will be even further below decent subsistence and have to be supplemented by some form of state or federal relief.

Refugee needs overwhelmed state agencies. Nurses were sent into the camps to immunize children; influenza, typhoid fever, polio, diarrhea, enteritis, and measles were rampant among the destitute families. "Children were reported dying in Tulare County," McWilliams notes, "at the rate of two a day, with 90 per cent of the mortality being among the children of migratory workers" (317).

With limited resources, the government camps furnished sanitary

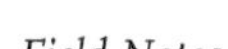

"The rains came": refugee farmers find cover

Spring flood in camp

LEFT: *Children playing in flooded area, Shafter camp*

RIGHT: *Wind damage in tent camp*

facilities, including flush toilets, showers, and laundry tubs. The majority of refugees in 1938, however, were still living in squatter camps, often improvised tarps stretched from their overtaxed vehicles to the ground. Yet the displaced continued to stream into the Central Valley, some 45,500 destitute Dust Bowl refugees arriving in spring 1938.

A day in the camps:

(1) Two boys—one 19, working & keeping a 14 yr. old brother in school.

(2) Several old men alone. Old men & single young men know they can't get help. They joke about getting married.

(3) Camp in field of cotton (next to Mexican's house with chickens) & married daughter pregnant 8 mo. & husband.

(4) Families in barn—one with boys who got first check and bought tent ($71) & going to move into camp.

(5) Others in barn—woman happy because has health.

(6) Embarrassed men who didn't want relief. Checks arriving just in time—with our first visit coming just when they thought they couldn't go on.

(7) Measles everywhere.

(8) Family in trailer with 8 children, all in bed with measles—even nursing baby. Want transportation back home.

(9) Heat in tents terrific—homemade stoves.

(10) Men bathing & trimming toenails.

(11) Cleanliness of women in camps. Few dirty.

(12) I sat on lard can to take case history. "We can't offer you any chairs but here's a box."

(13) Flour, potatoes. Pancakes—flour and water—& pies sometimes. Emergency food card—apricots, potatoes, flour.

(14) Mother & son in tent—he in one bed with flu. Other bed: springs & a few covers on the ground. The ground was very wet from the recent 5 weeks of rain—and because the sun & air couldn't get in. I told the

man if he felt he could, he should go into the sun. So he dressed & came out—very weak & feverish.

(15) Baby with bad eyes from measles.

(16) Pregnant woman & 9 children sleepy in barn with 2 calves to keep warm.

(17) Young woman in tent—so pretty & clean. Little box on floor with cold cream and powder.

(18) Call on woman who screams out: "You're too late! You're too late!" No food for 4 days. Mother and son in tent; daughter & husband & 2 children in trailer. Won't ask for relief but neighbors have said, Gov't man will come find them. Finally son goes out and steals from junk shop 4 radiators ($3.00) & when he sells them is arrested and jailed. Charged with burglary for breaking in place & felony for going to another county to sell them. (11 years in San Quentin.)

Sanora witnessed the horror of a family without resources for whom help arrived too late.

San Joaquin Valley, California, 1938:
Mr. and Mrs. Jack Straight at camp across the Tule River out of Porterville. Wife, young and very pretty and clean. Strong character in her delicate features. Husband young ex-Marine, who hated military life, and said we were first Americans he met that made him not ashamed of being American.

The wife is pregnant—her last month. The little boy, 3 yrs. old, in bed covered up because he has no clothes. Has no night clothes at all & no

After the storm

shoes. Healthy & pretty child, so good humored. Sat up awhile & then lay down & went to sleep.

They had had a child (girl) born a few weeks prematurely—weighed 6 pounds. She had baby at home during grasshopper invasion & grasshoppers chewed it while the mother was too ill to know. They took the baby to county hospital in Colorado & doctors said she might be infected by hoppers. So they proceeded to experiment on her with intravenous feeding, to see how long new baby could live without normal food—milk and water. Baby began to dry up. Finally they asked that she be brought home & her tongue was like dry leather. She was covered with needle holes & both legs infected where slashes had been made & were dressed. Baby was crusted with dirt & her sleeping clothes had not been changed for 5 weeks! Parents began to feed baby—drop of milk, orange juice or water every ten minutes. Gained 11 oz. in few days & then died of infection.

They came to California in a Ford to find work. Had no work or money until FSA checks. Landlady cashed first check & kept money for back rent & took trailer (worth $20) & locked it up for $2 rent. (Old lady has auto camp—prostitution.)

Wife went to County nurse & she was nice & sent her to superior nurse who was angry & flew into tirade when the woman asked for hospital care at birth because she always has abnormal births. Nurse tried to humiliate her & finally said, "Well, I suppose I'll have to let you in if she said so." First nurse also sent her to Red Cross for layette. Here she was about to get it & County nurse came and & told her to get out & said that they weren't making any more layettes for *these people*.

Now almost time for baby & mother is ill-fed & facing uncertain hospital care (may be emergency—which means go after labor pains start).

This couple was so nice, so much in love & the girl so lovely.

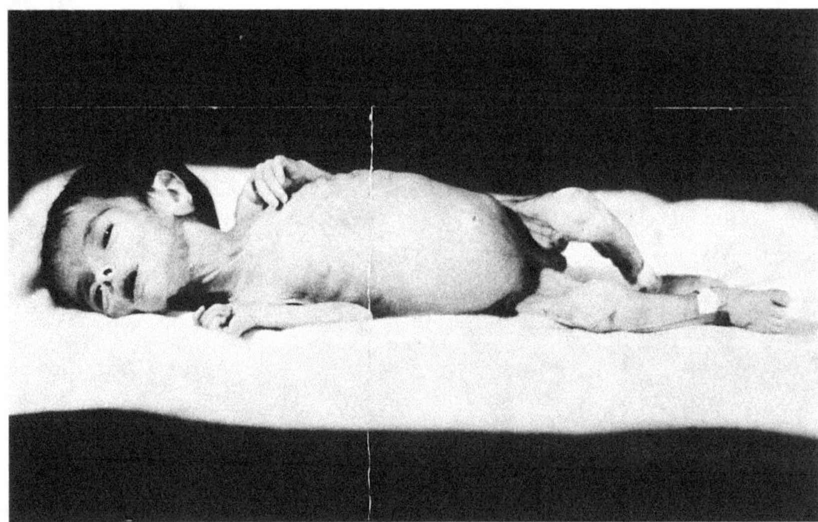

Starving refugee child

Cultural differences having to do with religion, race, and patriotism were often synonymous with differences in regional origins. Former sharecroppers and tenant farmers from eastern Oklahoma and Arkansas, for instance, brought fundamentalist and racist views with them to the western valleys. High Plains farmers and midwesterners were less likely to share these convictions and biases. Cultural divisions led to conflict in the camps, as Babb notes, particularly in matters of administering camp rules and activities. Political teachings were woven into the sermons of Pentecostal sects. Communism was the devil's business and "godless Reds" were his agents.

Patriotic sentiments, Gregory records, "channeled most energies away from the radical left, sometimes into the election campaigns of neo-populist candidates such as Murray and Carraway, sometimes into apathy" (160). In publications such as the *Bulletin of Associated Farmers of California, Inc.* growers played on these sentiments, warning of "Communist subversives" infiltrating the camps and organizing strikes. Fundamentalist preachers in the camps discouraged political engagement altogether. "Many of the churches," Gregory writes, "belonged to the Pentecostal or Holiness sects that taught that all forms of political action were wrong because they distracted from the pursuit of individual salvation. Worldliness of any kind was to be avoided" (161).

Religious extremism undermined efforts to improve health conditions in the camps, an issue that concerned Sanora and camp managers such as Tom Collins deeply. Sanora noted:

Thirty-seven varieties of religion have developed here in the camps since the Depression. Among the most violent are the Jehovah-nites (worst emotionally), the Burning Bushers, the Holy Rollers, etc. The most frequent call for the preacher and the followers come from others in childbirth pains but they have been called in for every kind of sickness. The preacher came, the followers, or neighbors came in, and the praying began. It kept on in varying degrees of chanting, moaning, praying, screaming, rolling about the ground, and even to the loss of speech, which results in the insane babbling, commonly known as "talking in tongues." This emotional ecstasy finally grips the sufferer as well, and finally when she is emotionally exhausted, she sleeps. This was believed the result of prayer. Unfortunately the victim had to go thru it all again very soon, but nevertheless something had happened. The visiting preacher collected his fee and went on his way, well out of sight when the pain began.

Peculiarly enough preachers arrived in camp with most friendly frequency, arriving in anything from Fords to bird egg blue Packard driven by God himself, as the sign on the car proclaimed and as he announced himself to the camp manager. Even the pennies of the destitute count up when they are camped together, and when the illnesses are frequent.

Callous as it may seem to some, something had to be done about these vulture preachers who induced emotional frenzies among the ignorant and sick people, and it had to be done carefully. The camp manager obtained a number of small booklets on first aid, sanitation, childcare, symptoms and treatment of common ailments, etc. As you well know, they all end in a sentence that warns the reader if the illness is serious, call a doctor. These books were made available to the people, and because they dealt with their everyday problems, they read them. They discovered many things, and they were encouraged to make use of these facts. A sanitary committee of women was elected. The camp manager bought from his own pocket, white uniforms for all of them. These women took their duties very seriously. They taught the others. They kept a check on the sanitary conditions of the camp, etc. The preachers were called less and less, and finally not at all. The camp manager arranged with a doctor to charge but 50 cents a call. The doctor was called when they could afford it, and the money went to him instead of to the preacher.

One day the woman's committee came to the camp manager and asked permission for a preacher to be called in for services. The camp manager said it was a matter for them all to decide, so a meeting was called. The worker-chairman announced the question. Someone made a motion; it was seconded, passed. It was that a preacher from any of the established faiths (Presbyterian was decided upon) be invited to come to the camp every fourth Sunday to preach a sermon in the government hall, but *that no collection would be allowed*. A man made a motion that the preacher come at 1 p.m. so that the sermon would be over in time for their Sunday ball game. The invitation was dispatched. The preacher never came, never even replied. This was the final blow to their belief in the help of religion.

Striking Workers, Angry Growers

Tensions between workers and the growers peaked in 1938–1939. In her field notes Sanora revealed her anticipation of impending strife:

I am afraid some blood will spill out on the green grass floor of the valleys this summer and next fall. It takes a long time for a farmer to make up his mind, but when it 'gets made up'. . . .

Tempers flared and tensions exploded when the CIO's UCAPAWA moved into the fields beginning in early 1938. The ensuing organized labor demonstrations represented the second wave of attempts to unionize field workers. The efforts of 1933 and 1934 in the Imperial and San Joaquin Valleys had made only marginal gains and resulted in the breakup of the CAWIU. The flood of dispossessed entering California with their desperate needs raised expectations that labor organizers might succeed this time.

The period of largest Okie migration, 1935–1937, had seen relatively little labor protest. Growers were at first content to have a pool of cheap, nonunionized workers eager for jobs. Yet their attitude changed quickly when it was noted that the refugees were to receive SRA relief funds for the first year they were in California. The presence of the FSA camps further irritated the growers. Despite their relatively small number and their function as demonstration models, the camps were viewed as evidence of government interference and centers of radical agitation. Things came to a head at Shafter in summer 1938. Angered by the camp's administrators, a group of cotton growers, local businesses, and the *Bakersfield Californian* publisher joined to initiate a political interest group called the Committee of Sixty, subsequently the California Citizens Committee, charging that government camps sheltered Communist organizers.

The angry exchanges of words turned to violence with the arrival of UCAPAWA organizers in the fields. Union organizers rushed to give direction to the momentum from spontaneous strikes, such as Babb's *Whose Names Are Unknown* dramatizes. The first significant test of their effectiveness occurred in fall 1938 in Kern County.

Union organizers demanded piece rates of $1 per hundred pounds of picked cotton. Growers replied with a rate of 75 cents and refused to negotiate. Governor Merriam's administration tightened the noose, eliminating relief payments to workers who refused to accept the growers' rate. Many of the workers ignored the strike and continued to pick at the going rate, driven both by desperation and innate suspicion of unions in general. Organizers went among the workers urging them to take part. Carrying signs inscribed with slogans—"Come out boys, help make your wife and children a living. What a husband that will work his wife in cotton for 80 ct. per" and "Come to our mass meeting"—workers, men and women, paraded in long lines along the fields, attempting to induce reluctant workers to join them. After some five weeks the strike sputtered out. Several hundred picketers were arrested and held briefly, but the strike had succeeded in inspiring among the refugee farmers a sense of their collective power. Perhaps for the first time they experienced the value of meeting to discuss what they would do, often without the presence of union organizers. The practice of running the affairs of the FSA camps prepared them for organizing protest demonstrations. On this point the growers were correct in their fears that the government camps were breeding grounds for dissent and labor activism.

Women in the camps brought food and encouragement to the strikers and participated in the protest marches. The Kern County demonstrations, centered at Arvin, boosted workers' spirits and strengthened their resolve. Several years earlier they had been a defeated people, acquiescing to the poverty wages, execrable housing, and humiliation of their degraded status as Okies. In late fall they returned to work at 80 cents per hundred. Yet many anticipated the next opportunity to make known their demands.

The opportunity came a year later near Madera, north of Fresno. In the meantime Californians had elected a new administration under Governor Olson, who backed the higher rates set the previous year by the State Relief Administration and appointed an articulate workers' advocate, Carey McWilliams, as commissioner of immigration and housing. In addition, workers who refused the lower rates paid by growers were no longer excluded from SRA relief rolls.

The conflict between growers and workers turned into warfare. As the strike spread to nearby fields, including Pixley, Arvin, and Corcoran, understaffed UCAPAWA organizers rushed from field to field attempting to direct the protest toward the goals they had set. As they had done in the 1933–1934 Imperial Valley strikes, the growers sent their "deputies"—hired thugs—together with the local sheriff's men into the squatter camps—the FSA camps were left alone—and to the picket lines with tire chains and pick handles. The violent confrontations ended when Governor Olson ordered the State Highway Patrol to intervene, but gratuitous attacks continued to flare up against individual organizers. The growers won the round; after two weeks workers returned to the fields at the same rate. Yet theirs was the greater victory, one that America's entry into World War II soon made irrelevant.

By 1940 the UCAPAWA had shifted its activities to the canneries, where its work might have a better chance of succeeding in the long term. A migrant workforce presents huge obstacles to labor organization because of the constant relocation of the workers. There were other reasons that unionization failed to take hold among the displaced Okies, the main one being the sheer surplus of desperate workers. The largest number of refugees were scattered along roadsides, in squatter camps, or temporarily housed in growers' shacks. Demoralized and disoriented, as Walter Stein points out, they were in no condition to learn union practices (260–261). More successful candidates were those in the FSA camps, where stability, security, and attention to essential needs such as health care and sanitation gave them opportunity and optimism that they might improve their work lives through collective effort.

The presence of union organizers offended some refugees' sensibility as loyal Americans. Racist attitudes intervened on the part of migrants from the cotton-growing areas of eastern Oklahoma, Arkansas, and Texas. Moreover, a tendency on the part of many was to identify their occupation as farmers with that of the growers, who had succeeded where the dispossessed farmers had failed. Given the opportunity they hoped to achieve financial independence permitting them to reconstruct their individual destinies.

Radical organizers and union officials were slow to realize the large differences among the Okies. Radicals and liberal sympathizers—many of whom came from Hollywood with gifts and money—based their efforts and expectations on the example of a relatively small number of Dust Bowl migrants, the farmers and small-town artisans. The legacy of the Populist, IWW, and Socialist movements in the Southwest, and in some cases actual union experience, fostered the notion that the Okies might turn sharply left, joining a vanguard of progressive industrial workers in the great factory strikes of the 1930s. A fraction of the refugees did in fact fit roughly these expectations. That the Okies represented a class of proud yeomen, however, who were not willing "to take it any longer" and would rise up in collective protest, proved unrealistic. Their organization was loose and voluntary; their strikes were often spontaneous, without the discipline of union leadership. The period of labor dissent among the displaced Okies proved fugitive. The more significant and longer-term transformation had to do with an evolving new constituency of "plain folk Americans," as Gregory describes it (xviii), that would put down roots in California, preserving their conservative cultural and political beliefs that in some cases made them ill adapted to California's mixed racial and ethnic heritage.

World War II scattered many of the Okies to the cities; some remained in the fields for the duration of the war, where the demand was soon met by migrant Mexican workers under the bracero program instituted in 1942. A few of the former refugees succeeded in becoming independent farmers.[8] The long tradition of corporate farms continues today in California's agricultural valleys. Nonetheless, the saga of Okie dispossession and resettlement continues its hold on California's Central Valley, where it is estimated that Okie descendants account for about half of the resident population of 2.7 million. The Okies' legacy is most prominent in the subculture of evangelical churches, country music, and conservative values, fostered by a collective feeling of pride of people, mainly old-stock Americans, who survived a national calamity and succeeded in making a profound mark on the American consciousness.

Drawing on her beloved High Plains people, Sanora Babb's literary legacy represents the hopes and expectations of a "saving remnant," in whom lies the potential for renewing democratic practices and progressive convictions. Her writing expresses certain ideals that fall short in individual instances but nonetheless represent the hopes and expectations of a democratic people. The lesson of the refugee camps was that lacking such ideals, a people lose their way and eventually engage even greater despair—alienation, disaffection, and ultimately the loss of freedom under authoritarian restraint. There was a risk that a situation of mass disaffection and despair could turn sour, with lasting consequences. The line between actuality and literary expression becomes blurred in such circumstances.

March 1938:
People stopped at a camp to take pictures of the way the migratory workers live. Big cotton grower (with several such camps on his place—tents, old boxcars, huts) jumped in his car and came over to the camp, lost his temper at the "intruders," asked what they were doing around there, and ordered them away. Threatened to break their camera, and demanded the film, which was finally given up. "The damn government helpin' these people has got all kinds of people out here snoopin' around." "I'm an American citizen in a free country and yet the government tells me I can only plant 500 acres of cotton instead of a thousand, and then turns around and *gives* these farm workers relief! Hell! in Cleveland's time they had a real depression and they got thru without anybody starving to death. They coulda done the same now. They don't need relief. What they've got is good enough for 'em—too good."

"All you hear is we ain't payin' these people no wages. These people are satisfied with what they're getting from us. They've lived on it so far—they can live on it now. It's good enough for 'em."

"Let me catch a CIO or any other organizer around here and I'll do more than break his damn head open. Just let me catch one of 'em."

Workers are listening, first surprised, and then angered. The grower went to the car and told the photographers to "get out, and don't come back, if you don't want to get hurt. Get out!"

A worker stepped between the grower and the car, first looked the grower right in the eye and said: "Glad 'tuv had you with us folks. Come back and see us anytime."

The grower was furious now. He yelled at the people—"Get back in your tents!" and got in his car, slammed the door and drove away. His reference only reminds us how the fascists always return to the past.

October 29, 1938—

Starting the 5th week of the cotton pickers' strike out of Bakersfield, Kern County. Strike is for raise of from 75 cents a cwt to $1.00 a cwt.

Houchin and Buerkle are big farmers in control of the Buttonwillow district. Last year small growers [were] willing to pay $1.00 but this year they have changed thru pressure upon them from the Associated Farmers (thru H & B). The kind attitude of the small farmer changed toward the migrant workers.

144 camps in Kern County now. Squatter camps not allowed thru stricter health rules. Most families now live in private camps on owners places, where the cabin is "free" rent but lights are $6.00 a month! In order to be allowed to live in a cabin, each cabin must show daily picking of cotton no lower than 900 lbs. This means at least three persons, more likely four. In most cases this means two or more families in a cabin. Average picker picks 250 lb. a day, 100 hrs. at 75 cents.—$1.87 per day. Many women cannot pick as much as men per day.

Pickers receive weight tickets at each sack weighing; then receive coupons at the company store (Houchin), with which they may buy needs. While some things are same price as in town, many articles are twice as much. This is one of the few places where the workers are not allowed to draw any cash at all until Saturday. By that time, tickets have probably mounted to as much or more than the pay.

Cabins in the Houchin and Buerkle places:

Rent is free (?); lights $6.00 per month. Will not permit use of any appliances. Some workers hide hot plates and use them because their light bill never actually runs over a minimum of 50 cents. Meter is seldom at the cabin.

900 lb. cotton minimum to [each] cabin: 2 and 3 families to a cabin.

In one camp of 200 people, 3 showers open from 4 to 7. Worker: "200 people can't take a shower in that time. They ought to put 2 doors on the shower so we could run thru. I'd ruther take me a bath in a no. 2 washtub than wade up to my knees in mud in the showers and not get wet even."

No furniture in the cabins. Crudest sanitation.

Irrigation and cotton chopping:

H and B paid 20 ct. an hour for both. Have to work 12 hours a day to get the 20 cents an hour. "Month hands" paid $2.00 a day flat. Irrigation: work many times in water waist deep and mud.

Worker: "I could only pick 200 lb. at 75 cents but I could pick 250 or

300 if I could get $1.00 a hundred. A man feels more interested in his work if he gets enough to eat and get along on. He likes it then."

"Them fellas are scabbin' all right; knees are muddy."

In Shafter there was an attempt to pass an ordinance to arrest any "loafer" who didn't have cotton sack straps showing on his clothes. These, of course, were the strikers.

"If they hadn't quit holdin' speaking here there wouldn't be no scabs at all in the camp."

"Why, I even thought we could smell the perfume of the flowers soon as we got near the California line. I thought this was Paradise. If I'd known we'd ever have to live like this I'd not come a step."

In order to keep the migrant workers from being able to register to vote, the Associated Farmers have a system of getting license numbers of cars. [They] keep a record of entrance time. If a worker stays in a county long enough to register (6 months) he is *let out* just before that time. If he moves on and asks for a job from other farmers, they look up in the record and refuse if he has lived in the county six months or the state almost a year.

Workers on Proposition No. 1: "If Proposition No. 1 goes thru, there's nothing left for us to do but git out our guns." Quiet one: "Trouble is we ain't organized to strike and we ain't organized to shoot neither."

400 scabs: men living with their families on private places afraid to come out [on strike] because they have no place to go and would be driven from the county because of "health" rules. Among the scabs, however, are many spies.

Several times arrests [made]. Once over [more than] 20. Again 84. Rumor that 30 injured.

While talking with the men in the [FSA] camp, Mrs B. stood aside awhile and finally asked us to come into the tent. She talked and then her husband came in quietly and sometimes they both talked at once, quietly, because he could not get a word in if he didn't. Finally I said "your husband wants the floor." She laughed and let him talk some. Her daughter and husband lived with them in a big tent. All out on strike, "all clean."

Mrs. H. is head of the camp committee and has to look after sanitation. Everything was fine save for one woman who was so afraid she'd "get something" she stood on the seat of the toilet and then would not clean it. Finally, when found she was only offender, she was simply told: "If y'er too nice to set on the toilet, then y'er too nice to have to."

All people talked to had progressed in the 8 months since I had seen them before from a bewildered attitude, one of not knowing a union, CIO, AFL, anything, to one of intelligent, reasonable and sound talk of their whole-hearted support; their realization of the fight between the Associated Farmers and themselves as workers.

Two stories of labor spies:

1. When the men were meeting and organizing, the women reported that one worker was seen hanging about the outside, listening. One night when the men wanted to meet and turn off the lights, one suggested no. That to keep the light on because it would certainly look suspicious in the dark, and besides, they couldn't talk in the dark as they should, seeing facial expressions, etc. "Do everything in the sunlight, that way you never get caught." Police began coming to the camp wanting to [identify] the organizers, the radicals. (The growers' definition of a radical is a "Communist." "Supposing I have cotton to pick, [the grower says]. Men come to work. I offer them 15 cents an hour. One man says he won't work for less than 30 cents. Well, that man's a Communist.") Police repeatedly turned away or permitted to come in without guns or hats. (Always afraid to come in without guns.) By this time they [the workers] know the spy is turning them in for talking organization. One day the police come out and have a warrant for the man who is the 1st [lead organizer] for car theft. The police go to his tent, check the license number of his old car, and take him along. One migrant, who had got on the local police force when he had got out of work, took another worker with him to the station when the night sergeant was along on duty. In the course of visiting, the men brought out some gin, and after due time, the police sergeant became drunk. This was the only place where there was a police radio station near. One of the men sent out the message to surrounding police

[identifying a man] wanted for car theft, described the car, license number, etc. The labor spy was arrested and held in jail several days and finally released, but he never returned to the camp.

2. After it was fully known that the worker was a labor spy and after the women's committee had reported upon him several times that he was also working at the nearby cannery, one day the police came to the camp saying they had had a complaint that a hog had been stolen from a big farm nearby, and that the blood had been traced to the highway and lost there. But they were sure the thieves were in the migrants' camp nearby. The manager thought this was not true but finally they went to the man's tent (they especially asked for as one of the thieves) and he was not there. Since he was at the cannery working, the police waited for him to come out after work, then they arrested him, examined his truck and found hidden in it a freshly killed hog. The man was taken to jail, knowing that he was recognized among the workers and he never came back to camp. While the police were identifying the blood on the car with even the possibility of a murder in mind, the man waited in jail charged with theft and murder but the latter charge was cleared up.

These men are themselves workers but [are] the type of Lumpenproletariat whose dignity and principles are lost, and would sell out their companions for a dollar.

A mother: "They make fun of us and hate us and call us 'Okies,' but if we have a war and they want my sons, they'll get the same kind of uniform as all the rest, and we won't be different then; we'll be good enough to fight."

"I was carrying my youngest boy when the last war came. He's just beginning to live now."

Old woman: "I have five sons, all grown now. It don't matter much about me livin' like this in the dirt, my life is about done. But I don't like my sons livin' like this, raising their children like this. This is a terrible way to live, it ain't decent. . . . I hope it can all be settled someway thru unions. I'd rather see my five sons fightin' for a union for a better livin' than fightin' a war, unless we had to fight against some terrible enemy. . . ."

We talked about the good feeling of not being alone, of sticking together, and one of the men leaned back on the cot and spread his arms out in a wide embrace. "Gee, it's a good feeling to be together. It's sure good to feel the love of one another." The word love lay in the warm air of the little tent for us to feel, in the unashamed and simple truth of his knowing.

Notes for a Novel

Little magazine editors such as Jack Conroy (*The Anvil*) and John T. Frederick (*The Midland*) welcomed the spare style and transparency of Babb's short stories, which, in the spirit of midwestern literary radicalism, represented in stark terms the harsh realities of the Depression. Editors of major publishers such as Scribner's and Knopf, who scanned the little magazines for new talent, encouraged Babb to submit a manuscript for a novel. The observations appearing in her field notes are fragments recorded in haste. They served to sharpen her eye to details and provide a substantive basis for her writing. In addition, it is likely that she made use of Dorothy's photographs in reconstituting scenes for her first novel. Critics have frequently noted the visual quality of Sanora's writing. The following are snapshot observations noted in her journal.

Be sure to put in novel about Negro committee with woman chairman—and conversation. (Suggestions to organizer instead of relief man.) Also, first meeting of white Texans with Negroes—group goes by house at night to pick him up for meeting. They like him. "He's a fine fellar." He "kept them laughing but he ain't just bein' funny—he's always sayin' something serious right in the fun. Notice it?"

Through Lancaster [California] at 10:24 a.m.
Elevation 2349 feet. Joshua trees & sagebrush & the long flat stretches of white.

Fruit-filled valley, Whittier, California

LEFT: *Figs, Fresno, California*

RIGHT: *Cotton wagon, Bakersfield, California*

Mojave.

11:10: Men still lying on the ground asleep around freight station. (When I came thru Mojave there were about 15 or 20 young men lying along the track on the raised platform. Some of them had their bundles. Some had nothing. A few were dressed in "respectable" clothes grown shabby (even carefully creased hats that give men a formal look). Others had on worn overalls, or unmatched ill-fitting clothes. If you've seen many "vags" or bums in your life you unconsciously know the difference between a tramp and a man sloughed off in present society's molt and decay. . . . I'm not sure a real bum would choose this kind of country for his "free and easy" life—the towns are small and far apart, treeless and dismal, squatting flat under the burning sun, on the bleak Mojave Desert—miles of gray waste—of sagebrush and strangely grotesque Joshua trees.

Tehachapi—noon

Kern County, February 23, 1938:
A girl leading (pulling, tugging) three goats along a road on the edge of town.

Four little boys—and then another group—walking along the road to the rural school. Two little boys had paper bag hats on their heads.

The small houses sit in the midst of a field—the small fields clinging to the hard feet of the Sierra Madre Mountains.

The sand—and the small thin rivers of the desert's edge.

The nostalgic charm of a meandering country road with narrow wagon tracks.

Sign: "For Repossessed farms of this district see . . ."
The scrubby little farms—then abruptly the rich orange groves, heavy with the bright fruit—the dark green leaves—the groves extending far over to the foot of the mountains with flowers planted between the rows.

The gray-green of the olive groves.

Bakersfield-Delano . . . cotton bales along the tracks.

Train man said: "Oh, we call them the 'Oklahoma coolies.'"

Man sitting along stream with only trousers on, and on all the bushes around him he had spread his washed clothes. He was sitting on a rock bare-waist and barefooted, reading a magazine.

Men thinking photograph of Roosevelt was one of [Governor] "Alfalfa Bill" Murray of Oklahoma.

Sanora Babb's field notes reveal the working methods of a writer not content to remain a detached observer or journalist. Like female regionalist writers such as Sarah Orne Jewett and Dorothy Canfield Fisher, Babb infused the particularities of time and place with an empathetic sensibility, fostering, to use Judith Fetterley and Marjorie Pryse's phrase, "an affective connection between the reader of the work and the lives the work depicts" (107). Such an approach, as Fetterley and Pryse point out, requires strategies to evoke an empathetic response while overcoming readers' anticipated resistance. In Babb's writing the resistance derives in part from the reader's unfamiliarity with the subject: few readers have experienced the mass dispossession of thousands of

Americans, the demeaning circumstances of radical *déclassement*, the deep political divisions of the 1930s. Moreover, complicated historical, sociological, political, and economic contexts with which most readers will only have a passing familiarity are embedded in the subject.

A certain advocacy, as Fetterley and Pryse point out, inheres in women's regionalist writing of the late nineteenth and early twentieth century. Advocacy also colors the radical narratives of the Depression era. The aftermath of political divisions that ultimately clashed with tragic consequences during the Cold War has left the legacy of 1930s literature mainly ignored, or, at worst, contemned. There exists, as a result, resistance on the part of readers, conditioned by dominant ideological response, to relive or have replayed those divisions, or to be open imaginatively to an understanding of the conditions that led to them. The memories of the McCarthy era when names were named and careers destroyed still resonate.

Babb sublimates the trauma, strong feeling, and partisanship of the years of protest and anger within a larger narrative of compassion that acquires impact through the emotional connotations of homelessness. The fact is that the literature of diaspora touches people across borders, race, and ethnicity. Migration is as old as humankind and as recent as today. "Many parts of the world today," Edmund Wilson noted in 1940, "are being flooded with migrants like the Joads, deprived of the dignity of a human society, forbidden the dignity of human work, and made to flee from their houses like prairie-dogs driven before a prairie fire" (43).

In the following selections from her documentary writing, Babb takes an empathetic stance toward her subjects while negotiating a space between the representation of particularized circumstances of an actual event and a larger narrative of a dispossessed people, the uprooted in any time and place. In her fiction she takes this a step further, shifting the center of perception from looking in to looking out from the perspective of the other. This shift requires the reader's willingness to approach the heart of the subject, which is the very meaning of empathetic understanding.

3 REPORTAGE

Make me feel *what periods you have lived.*

EMERSON TO WHITMAN

Sanora Babb's apprenticeship as a writer began in the typesetting room of the *Forgan Enterprise* (Oklahoma), where at age twelve she worked as a printer's devil. Her next job was cub reporter for the *Garden City Herald* (Kansas) before moving to Los Angeles in 1929. There her hopes of finding a newspaper job evaporated with the layoffs of the early Depression. After a period of unemployment she found work writing radio scripts for Warner Brothers' radio station KFWB. Her newspaper career was cut short, but she had opportunities to use her journalist's skills while reporting on labor conditions at the Hoover Dam construction site (1932), in the coal mines of Gallup, New Mexico (1935), and in California's agricultural valleys (1938–1939). As a writer of short stories and a frequent contributor to literary magazines, Babb employed literary methods—setting, dialogue, and narrative development—to give dramatic interest to her reportage.

"Migratory Farm Workers in California" appears to have been addressed to a leftist readership, perhaps a Communist Party unit in Southern California. A shared perception of social justice drew Babb to the Party in 1937. Like many progressives at the time, she viewed the CPA as the most effective agent for advancing workers' rights. Her participation was of limited scope, however, in contrast to Party activists such as Dorothy Ray Healey and Ella Winter. Like her friend Meridel Le Sueur, Sanora felt an instinctive affiliation with Party aims. With the exception of a walnut pickers' strike near Modesto that she helped to organize, she limited her political activism to the support of progressive organizations such as the Anti-Nazi League and the League of American Writers. Through the Progressive movement Babb was introduced to a wide circle of writers and artists, and like many in the movement she suffered blacklisting in the early Cold War years. Khruschev's revelations—at the 1956 Party Congress—of Stalin's crimes effectively ended her ties with the CPA but not her devotion to progressive aims.

In "Migratory Farm Workers in California," Babb outlines living conditions in the fields, the nature of farm ownership, and the circumstances that led the refugees finally to accept labor organization. In the camps Sanora was introduced to Tom Collins's innovative system of self-government, "Democracy Functioning." The basis of FSA camp governance under Collins, this rudimentary system of democratic participation met easy acceptance among the refugees, who otherwise were reluctant to organize along the lines of industrial workers.

In her documentary writing Babb sometimes achieved an unsteady balance between empathy for her subject and objectivity. Close enough to view clearly the lives of the refugees, she nonetheless let her feelings prevail in misreading their frustration and anger as potential for revolutionary action. Her suggestion that with proper "education" Collins might "accept the logic of communism" fell wide of the mark. Neither Collins nor the refugee farmers proved "educable" in the sense that they were able or willing to view Communist precepts as a remedy for their situation, which they sensed was temporary. What Babb observed in the camps was a rudimentary form of democracy reconstituted by the dispossessed farmers—even as their frontier forebears had embraced democratic practices.

The left hoped to join farmers and factory workers in common cause against the owner class. In their own minds the High Plains farmers *were* members of this class or hoped to be once the hard times were over. Few factory workers could hope as much. Nonetheless, CIO organizers, some of whom belonged to the Communist Party, succeeded in staging demonstrations among the refugee farmers that improved their pay and working conditions. Protest demonstrations together with the visibility that they received through the work of the FSA, including its photo documentation unit, mended immediate wrongs but failed to bring about long-term labor reforms on the scale of those won by factory workers through unionization.

MIGRATORY FARM WORKERS IN CALIFORNIA (1938)

Of the approximate 250,000 migratory farm workers in California, thousands are Filipinos and a fewer number of Asians, Negroes and Mexicans. But the majority are American farm laborers and ex-farm owners from the middle-western states driven westward by loss from mortgages and drought, and invited by the advertisements big farm owners have been running in the mid-west papers.

There are about 12,000 migratory farm workers camping in Tulare County in the San Joaquin Valley where I have been for the past month. They continue to enter that county alone at the rate of one hundred a day, from the Midwest.

There are three types of camps in the state in which these workers live.

(1) Government camps, of which there are only seven completed, providing modern sanitary facilities and wooden tent floors. These are "demonstrational" camps, and most of them are open only a few months a year.

(2) The private grower camps, operated on the property of [the] grower, with either free tent space, rented ground space or rented cabins, or tents. The grower furnishes water (sometimes five miles away) and poorest kind of toilets. The workers are usually forced to move as soon as crops are harvested. In some of the private camps, a certain number of workers are housed the year round at high rentals. In all these camps the grower maintains one or more camp spies.

(3) Squatter camps, in which the majority of the migratory workers live. There are now about 2,000 of these in the state. These camps are on private property without consent of the owner, and absolutely barren of any sanitary facilities.

"Without consent of the owner" means that the land is owned by an absentee, not that they are welcome.

While the small farmer is almost extinct in California, most of the ones existing are somewhat sympathetic to the farm workers because they have begun to realize that they are little more than farm laborers themselves. Most of them borrow from the finance companies to plant their crops, and the returns go first to the company. Sometimes the small farmer owes the company a balance. I heard one of them say that he had shipped oranges for three years and was in the red every year after hard work and sacrifice. He said, "I tell you, there's something wrong, and I'm ready to get my gun out if I just knew who to shoot." I also overheard an argument in a cafe, which almost ended in a fight, between a big grower and a small farmer. The big grower was angry because the small farmer was voluntarily paying 35 cents an hour to orange pickers. He said: "Eighteen cents an hour's enough for them; it's too good, they're not used to anything better. You're just stirrin' up trouble for all of us, you goddam fool!" The small farmer said: "A man with a family can't live on the wages you big farmers pay; it's all he can do to live on 35 cents. I'll pay 45 cents, even 50 cents if I have to. It'd be better for all of us." The big grower said: "If you got no better sense than that, there's a way to show you some one of these days. Wait till someone kills that goddam Roosevelt, and we'll show you what we'll pay these tramps."

In August and September, in the fruit, the migratory workers make the most money of the year. During January, February and March, the lot of them are at their lowest ebb. There is almost no work for any great number of them during these months, and since they do not make enough in other months to save for the three workless ones, they must either get some kind of relief or starve. Families who have been in the state a year or more may (with a great deal of difficulty) draw relief from the SRA. Those who have been in the state less than a year have had no way of getting through unemployed times until the recent federal aid through the Department of Agriculture, and this is a temporary grant, ending in May.

When I went to Tulare County, therefore, I was able to find most of the men and women in their tents, although they went out some part of every day hunting for odd jobs weeding spinach, picking scrub cotton and oranges (mostly done there by high school students of the surrounding towns). I was able to go into the country with a rural rehabilitation director at large, and on two days a week to help him interview farm workers for their relief grants. Since many of them did not yet know there was any help forthcoming, we went into the country searching for families in tents, old barns, sheds, any shelter they could find. This walking over the country or riding with workers was not a part of the work; the workers were to come in and ask for relief, and if they did not know about it, then they didn't get any help. The rehabilitation director went out to find them because he was sincerely concerned. In this way, I saw many families who had had no work, and were too weak and hungry to look any more. Some of them had no beds and were sleeping in old barns on hay or on the bare ground. One pregnant woman with nine children was sleeping in a shed

"Our daily bread"

Camp committee meeting in tent

with several calves in order to keep warm. They had no covers or furniture of any kind and had lost their car. Many families were lying in bed unable to get up. Many of them were on the last of their food with no way of getting more. Some of them had already received their first checks, and bought a supply of flour, lard and potatoes—their unchanging menu. A number of the people had to be forced to sign for relief; they thought it was charity, and kept repeating they had never had to ask for help in their lives. This was always the first thing the men said when they came to sign for relief in the office.

Under such conditions I expected the people to be in despair and hopelessness. It is true they were miserable and ill and almost hopeless, but they had not given up that there was no way for them to earn a living by honest work. No one was willing in a cringing manner to work for the low pay the big farmers offer. Those who went out and worked all day for 50 cents and sometimes less refused to go out again for the same pay.

These people are honest, proud and dignified. They have sensed very quickly the attempt to subjugate and beat them down to low wages and a precarious living in order that they will be glad to receive even the smallest pay. Without any encouragement whatever, once they knew we were friends, they spoke of the necessity of "getting together" somehow to

Sanora Babb with CIO organizer and child

OPPOSITE PAGE

TOP LEFT: *CIO hall, Corcoran, "UCPWA, Local"*

TOP RIGHT: *CIO camp*

MIDDLE LEFT: *CIO camp with ditch to protect from floods*

MIDDLE RIGHT: *Entry to CIO camp*

BOTTOM LEFT: *CIO camp guard*

BOTTOM RIGHT: *Milk delivery, CIO camp*

protect themselves and to improve their living. They spoke of not being treated "like human beings" by the farmers, the people in the towns, and other relief people. Their resentment, peculiarly without bitterness, was nevertheless pointed in the right direction. Their desire to get a just return for their work is strong in many cases to the point of a near-revolutionary state. They have brought their guns with them from the farms, the guns they kept for hawks and coyotes. But since many of them have already seen the vigilante guns or have heard of them from the ones who have, they keep them hidden under the mattresses, or tied securely hidden in the tent walls. They all say they will not live as they do now another year, and out of this talk among themselves has risen a kind of slogan they all use once they feel they can speak without fear: "This is the last year. Maybe October." It is true that many of them do not know what they mean when they use this, but it gives them certain courage. Others believe that, knowing actually no other way, they will have to fight their way out of their conditions. That is the only way they know "to get together."

While a few of them have belonged to A.F.L. unions saying bitterly that they have torn their cards up, most of them don't know what a union is, and if so, have no idea how to get into one, whether they could trust it,

and so on. The strange situation was everywhere, of these men wanting a concrete way to unity and not having anyone to help them. One of the men who later became a CIO organizer said to me: "All we know is to work, and there ain't no work. We're ignorant, and we need someone to help us, then we'll do the rest." They don't want "outsiders"—meaning people who do not understand the problems of a farmer. One of the men, a striker in the fruit [fields] a few years ago, hated "outside" leaders because in a strike where they had won their wage demands, the leaders held them out for recognition, which was not granted, and the fruit rotted and wasted. This man said: "A farmer can't stand to see a crop go to waste; we got the pay we wanted; maybe another year we could win the recognition. I tore up my card. If we had a leader who was a farmer he would have seen how the farmers were disgusted." This is only one instance of the farm workers' mistrust of the "city leaders."

Because they trusted me, I was able to talk to them and explain the CIO as a step. They all listened, asked questions, said what they wanted. I did not find one man or woman who drew back or hesitated. The only reservation was "I'll join a union if it is a big union for all—that's the only way we can do anything here against the big growers." They wanted their own men as leaders, organizers, but they could not see how that could be done when they knew no more than they themselves. There were already a number of fine leaders developed in the "D.F.S," which I will explain. Once these men learned of the CIO they went among the camps explaining to the others. One man even went onto the well-guarded and dangerous Tagus ranch, explained to a friend there, and that man promised to do work among the workers around him in the sheds, and develop another for the fields.

The question of racial prejudice had to be brought up because it is obviously played upon by the farmers [farm owners] to keep prejudice alive. One of the main difficulties already in the failure of strikes is the split of the (a) cannery, (b) packing, and (c) agricultural workers. In many cases these divisions occur conveniently with racial divisions. After discussing this with them, stressing the question as to whether they were fighting among themselves as workers of one race or another, or fighting together successfully against the big growers and corporation owners who were pleased with their squabbling, they seemed to have no difficulty understanding this problem. It was a fine thing to hear them explaining this to others, and encouraging friendly relations. When I asked the CIO to send someone to put a few days' finishing on the training of the leaders who have since become CIO organizers (willingly without any pay because they want to help and cannot wait for decisions about money), three men came: two Americans, one farm organizer, one teacher, and a Filipino organizer. These three were Party people, and they were so pleased with the development of the migratory farm workers there that only one of them stayed to fit the men with credentials and give them a few pointers.

The next night, one group met with a small group of Negroes, one of them a CIO organizer, and came back feeling very happy for their new friends. One of the new migratory organizers told me before I left that the organizing was going "like a barn fire in a high wind." Some of them already have plans to move into other crops for organizing, while some of them plan to stay there to continue to organize local workers. The plan is to become well organized before they move into the big fruit counties to the north: Yolo County in early May for apricot thinning, July–August for apricot harvest; Butte County for peaches in August, September and

CIO *labor organizer*

a little in October with both peaches and prunes. They will go through the present beet crop where they are, even the cotton chopping, and continue quietly organizing in preparation for raising wages and getting recognition in the fruit. Of course, thousands will come into the fruit unorganized and hope they will be helped in their organization there. They move back again into the San Joaquin Valley in October–November and December for cotton, and into the Imperial Valley in November and December for late peas, and spring peas in February. This movement of course does not absorb all the workers because there is not work enough for the ones who do move into these crops. But they expect strikes in the fruit and again in the cotton.

There are any number of reasons why a relief check or a job will not slow them up. The Jim-Crowism practiced against them and their children in school as "Okies" is one of them. There is agitation among the big growers to change the minimum legal schooling to the 8th grade. They argue if the migratory children are forced to go to school longer, they will not have any cheap farm labor. As it is, school attendance is haphazard because of inadequate clothing and food. Two immediate problems in the cotton country are (a) the 40% cotton reduction in effect next year, and (b) the invention and manufacture (at Fresno) of a cotton chopper, a

Gene Gregg, CIO camp

"Democracy Functioning"

small machine pulled by a tractor, which will put a great number of men out of work and stretch the unemployment period at this season. The farm workers are fiercely angry about this, and they say they will break them up as fast as they put them in the fields.

D.F.S

When Tom Collins was sent by the government to organize demonstrational camps for the migratory farm workers, he introduced a system of camp self-government, which he called Functional Democracy. The camps were divided into units, and various committees were set up with delegates from the units, the basic problem being proper sanitation. This, of course, extended into other camp problems: adult recreation, children's playground, planning and fire, child welfare, women's club (good neighbor's club), and agricultural department. At the top was a Camp Committee, elected by the camp. It represented the campers in their relationship to the management. All problems of discipline, order, disputes among individuals and groups, and all questions of a controversial nature were handled by this committee. The committee met at regular intervals for counsel and assistance.

This has been an important factor in keeping and restoring human dignity to these workers who were in danger of slipping into vicious attitudes because of their treatment at work. In fact, it was so successful that people in those camps now having moved to various parts of the state in search of work have set up their little "D.F.S" wherever they go. They make a point of approaching newcomers, explaining the "D.F." and helping them set up committees. Many of the camps are so small that the committees are dwindled to one, made up of the natural leaders of the camp. The work of the "D.F.S" in such circumstances has also changed and the men themselves have added new features. What I saw of them showed me the fine cooperative spirit this idea fosters among the workers. The "D.F.S" not only help one another but they help new families who are finding it hard to live. They bring or send many people into the relief office. Those who are working share their money, little as it is, with those who are not. The women take part in this as well as the men. While they are invaluable among the workers, they have begun to realize that the "D.F." is not enough. They wish to keep it, but to move into other ways, as well. The "D.F." men were the men who became CIO organizers, were the first to join, and tell their friends.

The "D.F.S" have also become very good at handling the strangling religious question in the camps, under the tutelage of Mr. Collins, and the problem of labor spies. They have done some quite ingenious things in getting rid of spies harmlessly but surely; I say, harmlessly in the sense of protecting themselves in whatever they did. The 37 violent varieties of religion developed in the camps since the Depression are a major problem. The preachers not only prey upon the people (women mostly) for money during illness, but keep them doped away from doing anything about their economic conditions. The camp committees take this up as a matter that concerns the whole camp. The worker chairman announces the question. Someone makes a motion, and so forth. It is usually decided that a preacher from any established faith will be invited to speak every fourth Sunday in the camp, but that *no collection will be allowed*. The chosen preacher is then advised of this. Whereas, he came often before, invited and uninvited, he has always failed to put in an appearance under these conditions. This has been a rather decisive blow to their religious illusions, and while violent religions flourish particularly among the more ignorant "hill people" from Arkansas and Tennessee (in the minority fortunately), the lot of farmers are releasing their energies in other and more helpful directions.

Tom Collins himself is a sincere, self-sacrificing hard-working friend of these people, and many of them, never having found anyone else willing to help them since they came to California, believe him to be their only friend. They are suspicious of others, but they trust him to the utmost. He does not attempt to be a "power" among them; he sincerely tries to help them to help themselves, and they know this. He has gone only as far as he has with them because he does not know another way, but he is extremely willing to learn. He is sympathetic to the Communists in their work, and agrees with their principles and the necessity of a change. His greatest disagreement seems to be that he thinks if the Communists used an American term such as Functional Democracy instead of Communism they would get farther with Americans, because they wouldn't have to waste time explaining away the foreign sound of the word. This does not amount to a disagreeable prejudice but comes out of the wide success of the "D.F.S" and the ease with which the farm workers accepted the idea and the term. I believe that he simply needs to be "educated" in order to become an excellent worker among the farm workers whom he knows so thoroughly. I found him very eager to learn, honestly willing to admit his ignorance or errors in thinking and to accept the logic of Communism. His faults are not those of a utopian but those of a sincere, simple person who loves the people and works among them in the best way that he knows. He realizes the necessity of change and the method of change. He needs educating to show the functioning of this method and the interrelationship of forces.

I should like to recommend him for this "education" and I feel sure he would be invaluable working among the agricultural workers, and developing leaders among them to further carry on the work. Once convinced that this is a better way to help the farm workers he will work in the same way that he has done in the past years to develop the little "functional democracies." He works now in constant opposition and watching by the large growers because of his efforts to better the lives of these people. He kept pressing for more relief until it was granted, and finally got a federal commodity supply where the farm workers may obtain food and blankets and clothing before their checks arrive and when they are used up. He has taught them the use of mass protest at the relief offices, and in many ways uses our own tactics without knowing it. Some concentrated training should make him very useful in a larger way.

While in the fields Sanora submitted articles on the refugees' plight to *New Masses* and *People's World*. Seeking a larger readership, she submitted her observations in a long letter, dated August 12, 1938, to *Harper's Magazine*. It is likely she had in mind Caroline Henderson's "letters from the Dust Bowl," published in *Atlantic Monthly* between 1931 and 1937. For reasons of length, the editors at *Harper's* decided not to publish Babb's letter. The unpublished report draws attention to the disparity between the fertile abundance of California's agricultural valleys and the desperate condition of the refugee farmworkers.

THERE AIN'T NO FOOD

Sometimes in the dutiful reading of school history books the student suddenly comes upon a sentence or a paragraph that leaves a bright and unforgettable picture of a far off place in his mind. Such an imagined picture of the rich and fertile Valley of the Nile remains in most of our memories. In the future when American names have aged enough for historical reverence, surely the beautiful valleys of the western United States will be irresistibly described in the same way.

From the south to the north, along the floor of the valleys, lie the lush green fields of vegetables, walnut trees, grape vineyards, fruit orchards, cotton fields, and the gray-green olive groves. In the distance, sheltering the warm valleys, the Sierra Madre Mountains rise, peaked with snow. California is the greatest agricultural state in the nation. Crops are produced annually in excess of six hundred million dollars. It sounds like an advertisement; it sounds like an invitation. To the farmers in the Middlewest who have lost their farms to banks and mortgage companies, during the depression, and been driven from their homes by loss and dust, it was an invitation.

There is a strange new population of 250,000 in California, and this number grows at the appalling rate of something like one hundred a day. These are the migratory farm workers. Thousands of them are the migratory workers who have been in the state for some years: Americans, Filipinos, Mexicans, Negroes, and other racial groups. The majority of them are dispossessed families from Oklahoma, Kansas, Nebraska, Arkansas, Texas, and other Midwest states, all scornfully referred to as *Okies*.

These people have migrated half way across America in the simple and honorable search for work and food and shelter. They even dream of owning a little farm, a small rich piece of magic California earth. Under existing conditions, this last must surely remain a dream. The small, independent farmer is almost extinct in these western valleys, which are controlled by high finance—big growers, absentee corporation owners and banks.

This means that the working farmers must keep on the move, following the ripening crops, and wherever they settle for a little while in trailer, tent, abandoned barn or shed, they are ostracized, they live apart, they are *migrants* and *Okies*. Against opposition, the children attend public schools, in a hit-and-miss manner, dependent upon the state of their hunger, the size of the holes in their shoes.

It is quite possible to drive along the highways, admiring the lush scenery, without being disturbed by the sight of one of these small tent-communities. Most of them are along the by-roads, and in the fields. A few of them are in the many-tracked mud of barnyards on private ranches where workers are needed for the duration of a harvest. When that work is over, the camps are more often than not torn down and the families are forced to move on in search of another place to spread their tents.

These people are not filled with any romantic wanderlust; they do not "like to live like that"; they do not deserve the comfortable, disposing remark that "they don't know any better," as you will hear people say who have never sat inside a tent and talked to them. These are men and women who have owned their own farm-homes, or worked on farms, who have battled the violent elements of the plains to raise the bread and meat of the nation. They came from what is commonly called "the bread-basket of the world." There is about them still the quality of the pioneer. They have the simple and sturdy values often bemoaned as lost. They are a proud, strong people, patient, uncomplaining, intelligent. They want first of all to work, to have a home for their families, to educate their children, to *put something by* for the future. These simple rights are part of the heritage of Americans; it is difficult for them to understand that none of them remain. Their whole lives are concentrated now on one instinctive problem, that of keeping alive. The work in the fields is seasonal, and even if they are fortunate enough to get work in these seasons, there are

LEFT: *Corcoran, California, welcome sign (1938)*

RIGHT: *California State Employment Service office*

Milk for children, Corcoran camp

Mrs. Evans, social worker

several months in every year when there is nothing anywhere. It means that in spite of their willingness to do any kind of work, they live in a state of semi-starvation, exposed to the weather, poorly clothed, suffering endless little wants whose answer they have before taken for granted.

In the little back office, which served for interviewing the applicants for federal farm relief, I could see through the windows of the double door the tight-drawn hungry faces of the waiting men. One at a time through the door, removing a shabby hat, hesitating, they sit down, painfully embarrassed. The answers were straightforward, quiet. Finally, there was one about food, how much food *have* you? The answer to this one was never easy. Every man hesitated, tightening the muscles in his throat and around his mouth, and suddenly began to say what he had wanted to say if there had been the slightest pause in the hurried questioning. "Well, mister, I never had to ask for no help before. I always wanted to do what was right—I was raised like that—but, well, I'll tell you,"—pauses—"my women and my kids are hungry. *There ain't no food*. I never wanted to ask for no help, mister . . . but . . ." All right. It is time for the next one. When a man hasn't eaten for a day or two, and has eaten nothing for months before that but flour-and-water pancakes and maybe a few potatoes, he finds it very hard to speak of his needs. He perspires easily, and there's an almost uncontrollable trembling of the mouth and hands. Sometimes it is hard to keep from crying, not from self-pity, but from sheer physical weakness and its reflection upon the nervous system. To a farmer, "cryin' belongs to the wimmin folks," and he'd rather "swell and bust" with trying not to than to let anyone see him "weak."

It is hard to distinguish in my mind the several thousand faces I have seen, but the composite of them all could be the small lean face of the Midwesterner, marked sharply with honesty and hunger, the last almost concealed by a stern and independent pride. One tent is almost any tent, one family almost any other when life is pared down to the core of its needs: food and shelter and clothing.

As nearly as possible, these uprooted people "settle" in small communities together, living in tents. Many of them do not even possess a tent, and these are scattered over the countryside in chance-abandoned barns, old sheds, strange shelters. Others earning a little money here and there rent wretched one-room cabins in auto camps, worse than the tents. Other families unable to find a space to spread their tents free, must pay for space in these camps at about one dollar a week. To a man who finds an occasional day's work at fifty or seventy-five cents, or with his wife and children together makes a dollar or a dollar and a half and uses up his precious gas getting to and from the place, any rent is beyond his purse. In fact, food becomes a luxury, and the three familiar staples, flour and lard and potatoes, are stretched over longer and longer periods.

It is not then a surprising thing to look into a trailer, cabin, or tent and find a whole family lying on the crowded beds, unable to get up from hunger. They are very quiet. The baby cried for the first day and then became still. *Hungry mothers have no milk*. The others had lain down first because they were too dizzy to walk about, and when they thought of getting up again, their bodies refused, and their minds had sunk away into a dazed half-world.

State relief deals only with people who have a year's residence. There are thousands who have come here during the year. They are the kind of people who do not want relief. They want work, and a more permanent answer to their needs. When they are forced to ask for relief, or are found starving, they are embarrassed, "disgraced." If the federal government had not offered the farm workers a little help, it is no exaggeration to say that thousands of them would have died of starvation. There was no other way. Though the F.S.A. is temporary it is bitterly fought by the Associated Farmers. This help just keeps them from starving, leaving them hungry days, and by no means, proper nourishment at any time, but at least a chance to survive.

It is difficult to know how one family, sometimes as large as ten or eleven, can live at all in one small space, on an amount of money per month which is only a fraction of what is frequently spent by some people for an evening's entertainment. The standard of such living drops to the lowest rung. The *furniture* is a dramatic symbol of the content of their lives. Beds: I have never seen more than two for the largest of families. A homemade table. A makeshift stove, burning as much as can be afforded to drive the dampness from the tent. One or two boxes for chairs. In most of the tents, I have seen a brave attempt to achieve that forgotten, old-fashioned "starched-up" appearance. One woman said to me: "I try to get enough water to wash one quilt every week, and keep the beds as clean as I can." Here and there a few little framed pictures tacked on a tent pole complete the pitiful effort to make a *home*.

The women wash and iron and cook under the most trying conditions. Water must be carried, sometimes only a short way, sometimes a very long one. The stoves mostly burn wood, and that means the tent is so hot when the fire is going that one can hardly breathe. When the fire is out, the tent is damp and cold. In spite of the difficulties, I have seen pans of tempting and delicious bread, corn bread and fluffy rolls emerge from these whole, battered stoves like a homely defiance of the tragic circumstance.

It is only natural that under such conditions of living, illness is prevalent. The surprising thing is that it is not more so. Even though many of them are now apparently in good health, the future is quite sure to bring out the results of undernourishment and neglect. A terrifying lot of children have pinched *old* faces and thin curving chests. Few of the tents now have dry floors; the rainy season has stretched over several months, and then the floods came. These people live on the damp ground all the time. It is almost impossible to dry out the floor of a tent, even though the surrounding ground dries out. Inside the dampness has caught and held the odors of living—a mixture of beds, cooking, clothes, bodies and illness, and permeating it all the covered smell of dank earth. The women labor to keep their tents clean and fresh but it is almost impossible with so many persons living, eating, sleeping in one crowded space. "I never had to live like this before," they apologize. "Some days as hard as I try to be cheerful I can hardly stand another minute of it!" Some beds are off the floor, but even then the dampness is unhealthily present. Many beds are nothing but mattresses on the ground and here the dampness creeps into the bed itself mildewing the side next to the earth. The nearest town dumps have provided a few persistent searchers with cast off springs, and occasionally a bedstead.

There is a continual epidemic of measles, mumps, whooping cough, scarlet fever, pneumonia and a few cases of small pox among the children. One little boy had infantile paralysis, another diphtheria. They had been admitted to the hospital but were sent home long before they were able to continue life in a leaky tent. If one child in a family gets a contagious disease, because of the impossibility of isolation, all of them are usually

Outdoor kitchen in refugee camp

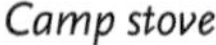

Camp stove

Cooking fudge in tent

in bed at one time. In one trailer, I found a family of eight children, all in two beds with the measles. The mother who had just recovered from them was sitting on a box nursing a very young baby, also feverish and broken out with measles. One little girl about eight, squeezed in bed with the others, was very ill with pneumonia. They had no food at all, and no gas for the car and they were miles from a town. As hard as the harassed mothers try it is impossible to give their children the best of care, and many of the ones recovering from measles and scarlet fever are suffering from badly affected eyes.

The era of unattended childbirth is looked upon by most people as a phase of the far past. Many of these women who have doubtless had their other children with the aid of the country doctor are suddenly forced to have their children without medical aid. The fact that so many of them live through the ordeal by no means proves that they have done so successfully. The few gaining admittance to hospitals are sent back to their tents after a few days. There is hardly a woman not needing treatment, even hospitalization, but somehow they go on with the daily drudgery, and when there is a chance to work, the money is so sorely needed the women go into the fields and work with the men. There is some opinion that these farm women have always worked in the fields, but this is true only in isolated instances. Farmers' wives have almost more than they can manage of their own duties.

It would seem that these people should be beaten with their despair and suffering, and the endless and almost futile struggle to keep alive. But nothing is farther from the truth. They have all lived better, even though life was a struggle enough for them, but none of them are resigned to the squalor and the misery of their present existence. They have a deep sense of what living in America should mean. They have been patient a long time, but they have begun to question their patience. Must their children grow up like this, hungry, ragged, unhealthy, half-schooled and scorned as *Okies*? They do not want another year of this living, and the courage and the hope with which they voice their determination prickles in the memory as deeply as their suffering. "It ain't right for Americans who've worked all their lives to have to live like this!" They are pioneers, but they pushed the frontier into the Pacific Ocean.

The documentary movement engaged writers as diverse as Ernest Hemingway (war veterans in Florida), Dorothy Parker (the Spanish Civil War), Erskine Caldwell (sharecroppers in the South), Jack Conroy (industrial workers), and Richard Wright (the migration of black cotton workers to northern industrial cities). A participant observer in the Depression era, as William Stott writes, "partook of the events he reported and bared his feelings and attitudes to influence the reader's own. . . . [T]his reporting technique responded to the appetite of the people of the time for lived, firsthand experience, and to their particular trust in the truth—the nonfalsifiability—of such experience" (178–179).

FARMERS WITHOUT FARMS

In the brief spring before the long summer heat, the great California Valleys are bright with new grass and flowering weeds, fruit blossoms, and the high color of oranges and lemons, ripe on the trees. Sheltering groves of olive trees are gray-green against the delicate white and pink of apricot and peach blooms. Nearer the earth the picked cotton plants are dry and brown. Grape vineyards are not yet green, and the prehistoric-looking fig trees twist their strange patterns along the fertile valley floor. Across the open fields, vegetables are being planted or tended by stooping workers; in another county they are ripe, being gathered in by bending, crawling men and women with baskets on their shoulders. The farthest range of Sierra Madre Mountains is pointed with snow, rising beyond the lower range. The air is sweet with spring.

"But you can't eat the scenery," a farm worker's wife said to me. "Even if it's 'most something to eat and you can't hardly enjoy the spring when you're hungry. But it is purty, ain't it?"

It's purty indeed, and rich with food, but off the road, between the orchards, in cotton fields, even in the little towns, the people who plant

LEFT: *Oranges ready for harvesting*

RIGHT: *Collection, Corcoran camp*

and tend and harvest the crops are living in tents and shacks and abandoned barns. They are hungry and ill and sometimes cold in the California nights. In every direction the low and almost hidden tents of the migratory workers' camps accuse the absent owners of this ripening wealth.

Of the 250,000 migratory farm-workers in California, including thousands of resident Filipinos, Mexican, and Negro workers, the majority have migrated from the Middle West, leaving behind them mortgage-lost farms, bank-claimed machinery and animals, dust-ruined acres. This is another great migration westwards in American history. The 1849 migrants came for gold; in an older America, they come for bread. They have stopped in California because the Pacific Ocean has made it the last frontier, because the climate is mild, and possibly because the greatest agricultural state in the nation seems a likely place for an uprooted farmer to go. Here he finds a worse poverty, low wages, unemployment, and thousands who have come before him living in the same conditions.

They have no way of living through the three workless months—January, February, March—and in the whole year, they average about three months' work, bare support for the time, leaving them starving and harassed the rest of the year. Only recently government aid through the Farm Security Administration has reached some of those families who have lived in the state less than a year. Even this is a small and temporary grant of two or three months ending with the beginning of certain harvests. Banker-backed Associated Farmers has already begun to fight the FSA, which came in only as an urgent measure to prevent mass starvation among farm workers refused relief from state and county agencies.

The full story of want and suffering and courage is beyond telling. When I walk along the roads, see the families in their tents, see them at their monotonous meals of flour-and-water pancakes and potatoes or beans, see them standing in line, hungry and humiliated, waiting to ask a little help, I think that surely no one can even *know* the presence of these conditions and not wonder at and question the appalling poverty and suffering of those people who produce the agricultural wealth which surrounds them but does not even sustain them. Yet I have heard the big growers, and the people of the little towns prompted by them, say, "It's good enough for them. They're used to it."

At the relief offices where the long lines extend out the door and into the street or alley, they do not talk much. They are hungry and it takes energy to talk. If they have made the mistake of asking at the state relief, they are wondering at the harsh answer, the cruel shoving and herding-out of the poor. These farm workers wait until the last food is gone before they will ask for help. Sometimes they wait two days without food, sure they will find work, trying to get up the courage to ask. Something in their strict Midwestern faces is unasking, unbelieving. A tall lean farmer apologized: ". . . just till I get a job. I never had to ask for no help before in my life. I always worked and wanted to do the right thing—I was raised like that—but, well, you see, my wife and kids' hungry. I declare, I've hunted ever' place for work, and there ain't no work. I only want this till I get a job, just so's we can eat and keep alive." These words are like the words of the man before him and every other man, repeating unconsciously his way of life, his stern sense of honesty, his genuine pride.

The face of an old man standing beside me was budding with sweat. He wiped his face with his sleeve and shielded his other arm carefully.

"What's the matter with your arm?"

"Blood poison in my hand, doctor said," and he showed me his right hand, red and swollen twice its size. "Week ago now, and it pains me way up in my shoulder and neck sompen' fierce. Terrible headache too." The sweat on his forehead again and he wiped it off.

"Isn't that doctor helping you?"

"No, he jes looked at it and said he couldn't do nothin' for me les' I get $30. He figgered $30 would cure. Fore that I went to the county hospital and the Red Cross both but they wouldn't treat it cause I ain't been here a year. I ain't never been sick a day in my life. I reckon I'll jes naterally have to get over it. Right now, my wife and me got only a mite o' lard left and I got to get a little sompen' to eat today if I can."

"What about your hand?"

"Have to let 'er go, I reckon. When a man ain't got money, he jes lives or dies. I sure worked hard forty years to end up this way." He wiped the pain-sprung sweat away and waited his turn.

Sunday is a special day even in a migratory camp. If there has been water and soap enough, it means a clean shirt and overalls, a clean calico dress. You can see them trying to tuck their weekday worries away to rest. The men are out in little knots talking, but they are talking about work, *the times*. The women, maybe, are visiting, maybe patching. The kids are jumping rope or chasing one another in a game. One Sunday in a camp I noticed a tent with the flap down and when I walked close I could hear someone sick, trying to breathe. I knocked on the tent pole and a shriveled old woman asked me in. Outside the sun was shining, but in the tent the floor was damp and cold; old dampness has a smell.

"I can't get it out," the old woman said at once, "I'm sick a smellin' the ground." Her grown son was lying on a bed without a mattress, the ragged covers pulled up under his chin. His face was flushed with fever.

"Flu, I guess," he said.

"It's too bad you can't feel the warm sun," I said.

There was nothing else in the tent but a camp stove, a skillet, a box, and bedspring on the wet ground. There was one quilt on the bare spring.

"It's his bed," the old woman said. "I made him sleep off the ground while he's sick."

"Have you anything to eat?" I asked her.

"A little flour and lard left. Wish I hadda handful apricots. I'd make Daryl a fried pie." She smiled at him.

"I'm all right mom. I don't feel like eatin' anyhow."

When I was leaving the camp, I looked back and saw him wrapped in a comforter, sitting on a box outside in the sun.

In a ditch-bank camp where tents and shacks fringed a muddy stream which served for drinking, laundering, and bathing, there were a number of single men living a kind of communal life, sharing a dilapidated car and whatever food they could buy from the earnings of those fortunate enough to get a day's work now and then. In one shack with a family, I met two young boys, one seventeen and the other fourteen. I asked if they belonged to the family and they said no, they were just "visitin' a minute." They had a few covers and they slept in the windbreak of other shacks.

"How do you get along when you can't find work?" I asked them.

"It don't sound real when you tell it," the older one said, "but sometimes we jus don't have nothin' to eat. There's no relief for single men or boys, you know." The women began to joke with them about getting married.

"We've been pickin' scrub cotton, but that's over. We hunt for work all the time," the younger brother said.

"O' course we'll go into fruit when it's ripe and maybe we can save some money. I want to keep Bud in school. I want him to be somethin'."

"I want to study to be an aeronautical engineer," the young boy said excitedly.

"He's gonna be one, too, if I can keep workin'," his brother said proudly. "If I had me a little piece of this valley to farm it'd be a sure thing then."

"Nothin's sure these days," said the fourteen-year-old. I saw where the worn soles of his shoes were broken from the uppers and laced together with fine wire.

These accidental neighbors, bunched on a ditch-bank, town edge, or in a field camp, are more fortunate in their proximity than the isolated families who, without tents or money, have wandered into a shambled barn and there may starve alone with no one knowing.

One middle-aged couple living in a decaying barn with their only possessions, an old camp stove and a few quilts, asked me back for a visit. "Come any evenin'. We'll get some new hay out of that field yonder and you can stay all night. Mother can make some mighty fine cornbread, but that's about all we can offer company."

These families are like thousands of others. Most of the tents are crowded with children. Most of them are clean. In excusing the box or lard-can offered for a chair, the intense heat from the tin camp-stove, or the cold, or the wet floor, the women say in their proud, unpitying way, "We never had to live like this before so it's a little hard to manage." And somehow they do manage to make good cornbread and rolls in the thin, battered stoves, to keep the one-room tents, with beds (maybe only a mattress or a spring or a pile of rags), a table, boxes, clean and in order. They manage to patch and make over their shabby clothes until they are more patches than anything else. They wash and iron under almost primitive conditions, and sometimes they carry the water for miles, even though the law requires water on the premises. They are a proud, honest, and dignified people, trying under the most discouraging conditions to continue their lives in the ways they knew before they were dispossessed of even their simple comforts.

The men seem to fare a little better in health than the women and children do. But to see a strong man, with nerves and emotions unhinged by hunger and worry, strain the twitching muscles of his face to keep from weeping, and sometimes to break and weep, is painful proof that none of them are for a moment free of the burden of their lives.

One day along the road a man had fainted. When he revived and sat up he tried to explain but he was so desperately worried, so weak, that it was hard to speak. He and his wife and child lived in an abandoned milk house, he had hunted all the time for work, he had lost his car and had to walk, and now they hadn't eaten anything for several days. It was terrible because she was hungry, because she had had no help, because now she was lying on the ground waiting for him to bring a doctor, to bring something to eat. There was no way to get either, but in his need he might *make* something happen. Then he had fainted. The baby was dead, but somehow the mother kept living. Young women quickly look like old women, living like this.

In this day of decorated hospital rooms, bedside telephones, and Cesarean births, it is shocking to find that these women are subjected to insults and humiliation when they ask admission to the county hospitals, and most of them, as was this woman, are turned away. Sometimes a sympathetic nurse advises an expectant mother to go to the hospital in labor; her screams may admit her as an emergency case. Many of them have no other choice than giving birth to their already malnourished babies without proper medical care, lying on a dirty mattress or a spring on the ground floor, with newspapers for sheets and possibly the help of the camp neighbors. Such a mother must suffer the heightened pains of an underfed body, and often find that she has no milk for her child. Other milk for babies and growing children is a rare delicacy, almost unknown. It isn't hard to understand how that in the worst places the death rate of children is one or two a day. The national average morality rate for children under one year is fifty-two per thousand. In the San Joaquin Valley, the infant death rate for 1937 was 139 per thousand—over two-and-a-half times as great. Refusal of the county hospitals to admit migrants has forced the FSA to establish the Agricultural Workers Health and Medical Association with offices in Fresno, Madera, Tulare, and Stockton. This will not provide medical aid to all migratory workers who need it, but it is a step forward in an almost unbelievable situation.

—*New Masses*, 21 June 1938

The displaced farmers in the camps, especially the women, were eager to share their stories with Sanora. Both she and Collins placed great value on recording the stories told in the camps, but Collins had a tin ear and was fond of devising his own version of dialectical verisi-

Waiting for milk

militude for the purpose—unachieved—of writing his own Dust Bowl novel. He made notes of humorous incidents and peculiar speech, sharing these with Steinbeck.[1] The speech and idioms of the Dust Bowl people were familiar to Sanora from her childhood on the High Plains, so reproducing them seemed quite natural to her. As part of her project of documenting camp life and field work, she encouraged people in the camps to write down their thoughts and experiences. The 1930s saw the appearance of road books by Erskine Caldwell, Edmund Wilson, James Rorty, and Ben Appel, who in their travels around the country recorded people telling their stories. Hearing the people speak, it was thought, provided the best window on a decade whose social and economic tumult sometimes exceeded journalistic description. The following first-person narrative is one of three that Babb edited for an issue of *The Clipper*, with little change in the orthography or grammar.

"WE SURE STRUCK IT TUFF": THE STORM

Author's note: When I was working in the California fields in 1938, and at brief periods for several years afterwards, I asked some of the women I knew if they would like to write down some of their experiences. They were pleased and enjoyed writing and later seeing their pieces in print.

In the year 1932, in the month of July, as we were traveling picking cotton, we had finished picking where we were and decided to go on about 50 miles. We pulled in to a little town by the name of Besley, Texas, located us a job of cotton to pick. We had got us a supply of groseries and the children had to get them some clothes the boy got him a new hat. Well the man who had the cotton to pick said we had better get all our camping things in the house as a gulf storm was reported, so we moved in and cooked supper. And about 9 o'clock the wind began to blow. The oldest boy said papa look to the roof of that house it is going to blow off pretty soon when the old man said we had better go to the barn. So we got all the children and started to the barn. As we left the house the roof left too and the house was tore to pieces. Nothing left but the floor. We got to the barn and stade there about 30 minutes and we could see that it was going to land there pretty soon. Well we all started to the door, the old man with two children, the oldest girl had the baby. And the oldest boy and his wife and 2 babys one four months old. We all got out someway. And we was trying to get the bunch together. The oldest girl said mama the baby is dead. O maybe not, let me see. Well the baby was dead allright. Then the boy said mommo, papa is killed. I saw a bord hit him about that time. I saw him. A bord had hit him and nocked him down but he wasent hurt much. Then some of them said mommo, Moncell is blowed away we cant find her, oh what will we do. But we found her. Her papa had dug a hole close to the fence and put her in it while he got the rest together. Well what will we do we cant stand here. We looked across the field and saw a light. It was about half mile. We'll try to get to the light, it is a house. I know. We all started. You kids all hold hands so you won't get blowed away and can help the other. We all started how we made it I dont know. There was tin and boards and all kinds of things in the air. We would crawl aways run away the wind would come in such hard puffs we would have to lay down and o how it did rain but we made it some way. When we got to the house it was a blowen and rainen and the house was a new house with a boy and a woman and man. But it had blowed off the foundation, moved it about 4 feet and we had to clime in the windows. Well the wind blowed all night and how it did rain but the sun was shining next morning and we had to gather our camping outfit up. It was well scattered and our bedding was ruined and our groseries ruined. We all had to laugh about the boys hat. He said I put it on my head when we started but the wind carried it away. He looked for 4 miles square but never found it. Well there we was broke everything runened. And I was sick had broke my sholder blade and tore three ribs luce in the storm. Well we loded up and drove about 2 hondered miles that day and we sure struck it tuff but we got by."

—"'We Sure Struck It Tuff': Three Documents of American Life," *The Clipper* 11 (October 1941): 14–15.

The small, independent farmer, in contrast to the absentee owners of corporate farms, is viewed sympathetically in the following reportage appearing in *New Masses* (May 23, 1939). Folk humor ends in surrealist nightmare as Sanora describes the ghastly spectacle of grasshoppers unimpeded in their march across the land, ravaging farm crops and city landscapes.

DEALING IN MAJOR CATASTROPHES

Down here in the San Joaquin Valley it is very quiet. But something big and terrible is happening in the quiet. Something big and terrible is always happening: the lives of the migratory workers—malnutrition, starvation, unemployment, low wages, tough looking men standing around watching for union organizers, sickness, no-shoes-no-school, living from place to place. This is just one of the big valleys on the West Coast; they're all the same. Imperial Valley is worse. But something new now, added.

As I was walking through the peaceful little park surrounding the County Courthouse in Fresno, I heard about it in another way than I was thinking. A young American boy was sitting on a bench. A Filipino crossed the lawn and sat down by him.

"What you say, kid?" he asked in his best imitation of our speech.

"Not much. I'm just thinkin'."

"Thinkin'?"

"Yeah. I don't know what the hell I'm thinkin' about." I walked slowly and listened. The Filipino listened. "I'm settin' here on my can waitin' for a major catastrophe." He pronounced the last words in quotes. "That's my trade nowadays, boy. *Major catastrophes.* Forest fires, earthquakes, floods. Only get a job when one of 'em happens. I'm settin' on my can again, waitin' for the grasshoppers to get goin'. I hope they eat up the whole goddamn country. I'm gettin' tough, boy, dealin' in major catastrophes. I'll get me a few squares and I'm on the bum again till somepen' happens."

GRASSHOPPER HUNGER MARCH

The insect invasion is in the back pages now, like an old murder, but the victim is still dead, the grasshoppers are still marching. And next fall workers will be talking about them when they're hungry. It was Saturday afternoon. The courthouse was deserted except for the scrubwomen and the state entomologists in the agriculture office. They were exhausted and sleepy, but we were going to drive seventy miles into the Coalinga district, scene of the worst infestation.

Past the green meadows with the great White Valley oaks and the Balm of Gilead poplars, we came into the desert—a low, dry floor covered with brown grass and loco weeds. The pavement showed black with the squashed remains of the 'hoppers. The car skidded. Fields of new cotton, barley near harvest, and flax in blue flower. Grain on small, dryland farms is half as tall as that on the big irrigated places. The fields are like islands in the wild lands. Grasshoppers kept crossing the road, going into the grass, toward the fields. The battle of the farmers grows more serious. Grasshoppers breed but once a year; they live a long time if there's sun and food. They are on a hunger march.

Poison bran is the most effective weapon against them, but the bran is running out, and it will be days before more comes from the Midwest. We stopped many times and walked in the grass, through the fields. At four o'clock the morning before I had watched a plane dusting poison over this area. Poison has to be broadcast before the temperature reaches 80 degrees. A few of the 'hoppers were dead or sick. Not many. It takes about five days to see results. Live ones were thick, crawling, hopping. It was like the earth moving underfoot as far as you could see in the short grass. They jumped up and covered our clothes.

THE WORKERS' COURAGE

On a big farm of thousands of acres, men were mixing poison bran. The crop owner was down from Berkeley in new overalls and leather jacket, city complexion. Two Rockefeller-Standard Oilmen came into the fields with us. They were all asking if the state planned to send out free airplanes for broadcasting poison.

"You could do that on our taxes alone," one of the oilmen said. A carload of Filipinos drove up and said they had come from Sacramento to see the housewives fighting the 'hoppers with brooms while their husbands worked! The workers mixing the poison bran smiled at me and winked. "If we ain't too dad-blamed tired, we'll study up somepen' better'n that tonight," one of them whispered. This in no way means that they are unmindful of the serious consequences of crop destruction, directly affecting their families, already living on the thin margin of existence. That humor is part of their courage, which might otherwise be justified complaint. It is part of that mighty spirit of working people everywhere in the world, extending themselves out of the poverty of their lives.

I rode back to the house with the Big Farmer.

"This is pretty serious," he said. "Something like this has great social significance. If it isn't stopped soon, it means hardship on thousands of migratory workers. Barley and flax harvests, and cotton chopping soon, and next fall picking. The company next to me uses thousands of workers. I keep as many of the best people as I can the year round. We've never driven them off the way a lot of them do. This the least we can do."

"THESE FOREIGNERS"

When I talked to the workers I had noticed their state accents. "Have any trouble with the Oklahomans?" I asked.

He smiled. "That depends on how you treat them. They're independent. Most of them are fine people. Naturally some aren't." A young county entomologist, ten years out of Oklahoma, had just been smugly telling how he hated the Oklahomans, all drunkards, fighters, thieves; in fact how he hated the Fresno Indians (Armenians), the Googoos (Filipinos), the Negroes, the Mexicans, the Rag-Heads (Hindus), the Eyetalians, Japs, Chinks.

"Do you like Hitler?" I asked him.

"No, I hate him too."

"You'd better think where we Americans came from or some local Hitler will sneak up on you."

"Well," he said, "I'd help in a purge of these foreigners out here."

"I think I'll walk over to the camp, if you don't mind," I told the farmer.

"Go right ahead, but if you've never been in one before, don't expect too much." I've been in so many I don't expect anything unless it's a government camp. You can tell the difference miles away. A quarter of a mile down the road the workers were living in a small group of corrugated iron shacks. Children were teeter-tottering on old tree stumps uprooted in the yard. Seven or eight women came out to "visit."

"These old tin houses are gettin' so hot we can't hardly stand 'em," a woman said. Grasshoppers were thick in the yard. "Now it's these pesky things." She shook them off her dress. "Eat up everything in sight. Hungrier'n we are." She laughed at her joke.

"That's goin' some," another woman said dryly.

"This a worryin' time, I'll tell you. You think these folks from the state can stop 'em? What next, I wonder?" I remembered being in the fields last spring when the floods came. I asked them how they liked the place.

"Not fit to live, but anything's better'n movin' all the time. We just about manage to eat and sleep. Sometimes I say to my husband, what in the world we livin' for any more? Can't look ahead, that's sure as death."

"Look at these blamed 'hoppers!" another woman said. "It's scary. I been wakin' up in the night imaginin' they could eat us all up if they took a mind to."

CHANGING THE TUNE

As if natural problems of fighting this strange menace were not enough, a diversity of interests delays work whose effectiveness depends upon quick action. Standard Oil owns the land. It is leased to big farmers, big cattle and sheep men, and rented to small farmers. Standard Oil gave the state permission to dust the wild lands, but the cattle and sheep men withheld theirs, fearing the poison. If machine dusting is used there is little or no danger to animals and birds, but many farmers are using their men to scatter by hand. Big farmers are worried about their crops but are reluctant to cooperate with the state in dusting the surrounding grassland. Obviously one without the other is useless. There is a shortage of men; workers are in other parts thinning fruit, harvesting vegetables. Associated Farmers, Inc. is calling for men from the CCC and WPA, agencies it has persistently fought to destroy. How feeble these men's concern for the state of the economy when *they* need help! A few thousand hungry men more or less—well, you can't afford to be sentimental. A few thousand acres, dollars, in danger—that's a horse of another color! Some place in all this cross firing, the small farmer is desperately worried about his crop. I walked with one of them into his barley. The edge was frayed clean, and far into the field every stem held as many insects as could crowd on its surface.

"You might say, now, my crop is a goner," he said. "Already stunted from lack of rain this year, but I was hopin' to get a little harvest, maybe enough to pay off the loan on it. I'll do well now to pay my rent to the big fellows—" he waved toward the Kettleman Hills, thick with oil derricks. "They say there's oil under this whole valley, so this small farmin' is a kinda fly-by-night affair. They say every well sunk costs around a hundred thousand dollars. Look at 'em! No place in the world for the little man any more. No difference much between us and these poor workers movin' through every crop." We spoke for a while about this, then he said: "Just to show you now, I'm willin' to pay $1 a hundred for cotton picking, one year I coulda paid $1.10 and still made a profit. A man can't live on less, and you get real work when you pay fair. But what happens? They're bigger'n we are. They say pay 75 cents. What can you do?"

A MAJOR CATASTROPHE

It is quiet out here in the fields save for the small, ominous sound of millions of grasshoppers chewing. It is hard to believe that something is happening on the still landscape which may ruin many small farmers, bite into the big company- and bank-owned farmers, creating added suffering for thousands of migratory workers. It is hard to believe because everything looks the same. But you can't put your foot down in a space clear of 'hoppers. I stood still and watched them: they are young, no more than an inch long, and their wings are showing. They are not the intensely migratory type, they are sluggish flyers whose weak wings seldom carry them into the air currents. This much is good. Neither do they move instinctively in one direction, unwilling to turn aside at any obstacle—a point that worried farmers and towns in the line of the march. They crawl steadily along, hopping some, and their big expressionless heads give them a purposeless look; but their saw-toothed legs moving over the miles an inch at a time, on a wide front, seventy-five miles deep, make you fearful of their instinctive determination. They march into a town, and all the giants above them, the machines roaring over them, cannot stop them. They are billions strong. They eat the lawns into the earth, the flowers and the vegetable gardens, and they move to other crops, to other towns—unless they are destroyed soon. If the farmers cannot handle the work themselves, the state plans to use CCC boys, WPA workers to fight the 'hopper invasion. The sheriff just told me he intends to take the prisoners out of jail. The next weeks will show whether or not this is a major catastrophe—now, and in all its subsequent hardships for the small farmers and the migratory workers dependent on this lap of their journey to get them through the workless months. If the young man sits in the park long enough to get vagged, he'll again be pursuing his depression job.

—*New Masses*, May 23, 1939

Sanora made friends among the migrant workers; her natural warmth and sincerity put people at ease. The intimacy that often developed problematized her role as journalist and novelist. It was difficult at first, she discovered, to gain the trust of the people in the camps. She described a visit to a family from Oklahoma during a rainy day when they were not able to go into the fields:

When we left they said they wished we didn't have to go because it was like visiting with old friends. That made me feel very happy. These people don't say things they don't mean, in fact, they won't say much of anything unless they think they can trust you.

The actual events of that time are long past. Yet Sanora's working journals, reportage, and short stories drawn from her FSA experiences have more than historical interest. In our time, when more than a million Mexican seasonal workers plant and harvest California's agricultural valleys and skilled American workers lose their jobs to out-sourcing, forcing them to confront similar struggles to survive with dignity, we need for our own day literary witnesses to the time and events. The worker-writers, journalists, documentarians, and social scientists of the 1930s—Sanora Babb, Erskine Caldwell, Jack Conroy, Pare Lorentz, Tillie Olsen, James Agee, Paul S. Taylor, Carey McWilliams, Walker Evans, Dorothea Lange—present models for a new *littérature engagée* that transposes conditions of social injustice—dispossession, hunger, sickness—into narratives of human endurance and dignity.

The 1930s brought these conditions into sharp focus. The endurance and resilience of the dryland farmers drew Sanora Babb to write about them, how they held on to things—their sense of home, their family, memories, and personal dignity—out of sheer stubborn resolve. Their dream had been rural ownership and independence. The new social frontier of market capitalism altered traditional farming practices, however, focusing them on cycles of business expansion and recession controlled by distant markets, government policy, and world weather conditions. The fate of the farmer-refugees was to be caught between a fading dream and the reality of speculative economic forces that dictated the price of crops and livestock. The creation of a class of landless wage earners who sought uncritically mass-market-produced culture and consumer goods conflicted with long-held convictions—personal autonomy, frugality, resourcefulness, and independence. What remained unaltered, however, was a conservative faith in hard work, individual initiative, and moral strictures.

In late spring 1938 Sanora wrote to her sister, Dorothy, in Los Angeles about her work among the dispossessed refugees in the camps. The letter makes clear her intimate, close-up relationship with the people whose lives she portrays in often shocking circumstances. To strike a balance between the empathetic concern she felt for her subjects and a critical interest in exploring the social dislocation and pauperization evidenced in their condition was resolved by aligning herself as a writer with the people who embody the power to change society should they choose to.

At the conclusion of the letter, Sanora mentions a visit by John Steinbeck to an FSA camp (probably Arvin) to research a novel on the Dust Bowl refugees. Accompanying Steinbeck was the photographer Horace Bristol. Their joint documentary effort to publicize the plight of the Okies in *Life* magazine never materialized. Steinbeck's *Grapes of Wrath,* which appeared the following year, however, brought nationwide attention to the refugees, sparking controversy and prompting governmental investigation of conditions in the fields.

Porterville, California
May 1938
Dear Dorothy,
. . . [*first page missing*]

Since we worked hard for twelve hours among the camps, and walked many miles between the camps in the country, I thought I would not be able to stand such a day. But I never felt bad once during the day and even when I got home I was physically tired but so filled with everything I had seen I stayed up and worked till midnight. Walking in the country is so much nicer anyway than walking in the city on the pavement. I talked to over 150 families and many more besides whom we didn't have to see this time about relief. The first thing I felt of course was the horrible way they have to live in tents, mostly without floors, one room, with home-made stoves, terrific heat from the stove in the tent, beds on the ground, or a spring or mattress on the ground, filthy covers, because although I saw only two dirty families, there is no way for the clean ones even to wash their heavy covers. They have to be careful with the little water they are allowed. The thing that perhaps impressed me even more than that is the courage of the people living under such conditions. They are all very proud, and several of the new ones simply had to be pressed to accept relief because they had children and were hungry and there is no more work here now. They'd say, "We've never had to ask for anything before, and we won't now. We'll find some work if there is any." They say that when they are weak with hunger, and there is nothing left to eat. None of them have more than flour and potatoes. The women make pancakes from flour and water, and sometimes when the check comes (all the way up to $30 a month for families with 9 and 10 children!) they buy a little fruit and make pies. They all try to keep lard too. They have no clothes except rags and when the women can get any material they make cotton dresses for the children and themselves and shirts for the men. They were all so clean, the dresses were washed and ironed with that "starched up" grandmother look. Two families were very dirty—the children were dirty and uncombed, and the tent was a sight! When I wanted to take pictures of the twin babies, the mother flew about to wash their faces and wanted to change their clothes. Finally she and the father decided to have their pictures taken with the twins, and they were obviously pleased. I told them I would send them the picture. I am worried about it because they wanted it taken in the tent (and so did I) and it was so dark, it may not show up very well. What big families they all have, because they are very poor and uninformed to know anything about birth control, and couldn't afford it if they did. About every third or fourth woman had just had a baby or was pregnant. They have them without doctors on their dirty beds, with newspapers under them, and somehow most of them live—babies and mothers. Some of them don't—some of them really die of starvation, and I'm surprised more don't. I don't see how people live for months and years on flour and water and potatoes and lard. They look amazingly well for all that. None of them complained. They all say—"Oh, we got by," or, "We'll get work soon." But the work in the cotton is all over now. This is the last day even of picking scrub cotton. Several families had been doing that, and altogether had made only a $1 or $1.50 a day. They want to work, and they don't like relief. Tom Collins explained to them that it isn't relief in the way they feel it. Every cotton farmer here is guaranteed by the government 9 cents a lb. for his cotton and can sell it for only about 5 cents. He then receives a check from the government for the balance. Tom Collins tells these people that they sell their labor for 50 cents and

$1 a day, and this monthly check merely tries to make up the difference. Of course, it doesn't even do that but it makes them feel better. Some of them have had one check, and will get one or two more, then this help ends. What they will do then, I don't know. Work will open in fruit in August and September, but there are many more people than there is need for them. There is no work anyplace in these months, except for a handful of people.

After seeing many people, we thought we had finished, and started to walk toward town to another camp along the way, and would catch the bus there. We walked about a mile and came to a fruit stand, and the family there told us about a family in a trailer in a field about 5 miles back—8 children, all down with the measles, no food for days. We walked back to Farmersville, and got a migrant to drive us out and we began to hunt for the family. We found them, and then we couldn't help them because they had been in the state over a year. The (California) State Emergency Relief Administration (SERA) has to take care of those cases and you have to be a corpse before they'll help. Anyway, the man said he just wanted to get back home in Oklahoma, and Tom Collins told him that the SERA would gladly give him transportation. They do that in order to get them out, and it wouldn't take much for them to drive back on. I went in the trailer, and it was so hot with the homemade stove going. There was no free space except a path to the bed a foot wide and 3 feet long. Seven children were in two beds, the mother was sitting on a box nursing the baby who was also broken out with measles. (In fact, every child we saw had either just had the measles or had them now—pneumonia, colds, etc.) One little girl was very sick, and the mother was afraid she has pneumonia, which is a rather usual combination with measles, and usually fatal. They all looked so miserable, poor little kids. One boy 16 couldn't even raise his head to look. When I told her they could get money for transportation back, she was so glad, and said she thought they'd be well enough in a week to start. The man was so happy, he followed us out to the car and kept thanking us. In that same camp, which was only a small one, we found a new family who had just been in the camp a few days, and the man had earned a few cents chopping wood, but that was over. There was another couple with them, and they all looked so nice. The men were evidently white-collar workers before. Both women were pregnant, and they had nothing left but flour. They didn't want relief, and they had to have it thoroughly explained first. They were so embarrassed at first, but before we left they felt all right about it, and were awfully happy to be able to look forward to a check, and to have the emergency food card which would let them get some flour, potatoes and apricots. They had a little girl too about 5.

(Have to stop and leave now. Something nice just happened. An old man who helps the woman hotel manager here a little, just brought me a big piece of angel food cake—the best one I ever tasted. I was surprised, and needless to say, pleased.)

You said you were afraid if you saw them in these pitiful living conditions, you'd feel hopeless. I don't think you would. When I heard about them, I thought so too. When I met them and talked with them in their tents, I came away feeling almost happy to see that people can be so brave in the face of almost unbearable living. They are, as you said, heroic. They are like the people of Spain, and of China: they are the "salt of the earth" kind, the honest, direct, patient people, who have worked hard all their lives, owned their homes, and farms, or worked on them and lived decently at least. They are the real descendants of the American pioneers, and if you'd see the spirit in them, you'd never cease to wonder. They live horribly, but their tents and barns and hovels are clean. They look for work every day. They talk and smile, and they have a native intelligence far above that section of the lower middle class just "above" them who have been drugged into stupidity. Many of them say, "This is about the last year," and you know what they mean. They don't say it in recklessness or anger but in patience and determination. I'm afraid it won't be that soon, but they've been driven from one place to another, they've seen the vigilante guns of this fascist state, they won't see their wives and their children starve forever. Here is what an SERA official here said, who is also a member of the big farmer group: "You know what ought to be done to these people coming in here from other states: we ought to dam up all the rivers in California and drive them in them." It is hard to imagine people are like that, but they are. The maid who cleans my room is a late-middle-aged woman, a former high school teacher from Kansas. She said to me this morning: "This is still in the United States of America but they don't act as if it were. People have a right to come here to look for work and a warm place to live, as well as the tourists who have money to spend, but they want only the last."

I'll tell you a little of what I did while I was in the country the last two days. Tuesday morning, Mr. Collins let me help him take applications in the office at Porterville, and one day next week I will do this by myself, from 3 to 5. It is a good chance to talk to people, because they do not know I want to write of them. I don't want them to think I am peering in on their wretched lives. I think this experience was almost as touching as visiting them in their homes. Only men came, and every one of them was embarrassed to ask for help, saying they never had to do that before. It is a terrible thing to see a crowd of hungry men waiting for a little help. These men yesterday were really hungry. The very last of the work picking cotton ended several days ago, and for many of them, eating also ended. We took one applicant at a time (in the back of the SERA offices), and the rest stood outside looking in the glass waiting their turns. We didn't have a man who wasn't weak and pale, lips and hand trembling from real starvation. They are very proud and try to cover their need. One of the questions is, how much food have you now? The answer was always the same: a pause, and then, "Well, mister (or missus), we haven't got none. It give out on Saturday (or whatever day). I sure hate to ask for anything, but my woman and my kids are hungry." They never say they are hungry. After we had given one man a food card, he told us he was so weak he could hardly stand. They will receive checks in about two weeks or less, but we can give them a food card and they can get food at once. No other relief is as immediate, and when these people are hungry, it is a good thing. Some of them were too late to get into the commodity store for food, and I told them to go to the county welfare and explain and get a little something for supper, but they all said they would wait until the next day.

After that, we went to visit families—new ones who need help, or a second call to see the ones who have received the check, so that they will receive another, next month. Even the town of Porterville has several camps—mud holes right in the city limits. We saw many people at dinner time, and some of them asked us to eat. "We haven't got much, but you're sure welcome." Flour-water pancakes (our old Baca County menu) and potatoes. The ones who hadn't food were just sitting, or getting ready for bed. They go out every day hunting for work and sometimes a few of them get an hour or two tying spinach. We had to hunt all over the country for families in old barns and tents and trailers, or any old vacated shelter. One family in a barn said if we got caught in the country, we could stay at their place; they'd get us some nice fresh hay and a clean blanket for each of us. Most places with children, and few haven't, are down with measles, or have just got up.

Yesterday, it was raining so we couldn't go into the country again because it means wading water. Mr. Collins would, but there was enough to do in town. When we finished we went to visit a family from Oklahoma and stayed about an hour and a half. They were such nice people and had eight of the best-looking children: 6 boys and 2 girls, all clean and bright looking. When we came in they told us: "Everybody in camp was talking about you folks this morning; said you worked day and night and in the rain, and are the only case people who are human beings." (Of course, I don't deserve this, even though I was there the night before, but it shows their feeling.) Their bedding was wet from the leaky tent and they had piled things up in the dry part and we all sat there. The woman was patching. The clothes are more patches than anything else. They wanted to give us a rag rug she had made of the rags they couldn't wear. It was very pretty, but they need it themselves. They said it would be to remember them by. They made some boiled-over coffee, and we all had some and talked together. When we left they said they wished we didn't have to go because it was like visiting with old friends. That made me feel very happy. These people don't say things they don't mean, in fact, they won't say much of anything unless they think they can trust you. I took a picture of them, and I surely hope it is good. The smallest boy, about 5, was surely cute. He was bashful, and kept hiding his head, and looking at us shyly. Finally he felt all right and talked some. When I looked at him, he would laugh and hide again. He had on some little coveralls, and all toes were out of both shoes, no stockings.

These farmers are a better breed than some of the regular migratory workers who've been here a long time. We saw only a few of them, and some of the men (alone) look pretty vicious. They have been sloughed off of society too long, and have become lumpenproletariat. These, however, are in the minority. The people from Kansas, Nebraska, and Oklahoma are a higher type than the ones from Arkansas, who are more ignorant and backward. You know how they live back in the hills, and it is no wonder they are like they are. They certainly have a speech all their own. One little Arkansas boy showed me a pup someone had thrown out of a truck going by breaking its legs; they had got him well, and he was busily chewing a piece of stove pipe under the bed, cutting his teeth; the little boy said, "Don't he look like a bar (bear)?" Many of them, the sharecroppers, are clean, and know what is happening to them. A few of them from back in the hills have to be taught the simplest kind of sanitation, and they are suspicious of everybody, and incredibly ignorant. Most of the people are from Oklahoma, then Kansas and Nebraska. They keep house in their tents in that old-fashioned "starched up" way. These people have a special appearance belonging to the midwest and of course their ancestry: they are nearly all lean, strong people, with straight honest eyes and small faces. They are friendly and hospitable if you are a friend.

I have already seen a large number of families. One of the worst was in the country, in a small trailer, which contained two beds, a small table, a homemade stove, a box. Tom Collins stayed outside with the man and I went in to see the mother and children. Seven of them were in the beds, lying cross-wise, with measles and a temperature, one with pneumonia. The mother was nursing the baby, broken out and fire red with measles. The poor woman was worn out, and they hadn't had food for days. Several people had told us about them, and we had hunted from camp to camp, and finally when we had walked a mile out of town to another camp and on our way home, a family at a fruit stand told us where they were—5 miles back. We walked back to town and got one of the men we knew in the camp to drive us out. Tom Collins has no car now and goes on buses, then walks; for the long distances, he hires the migrants to drive him. We visited a number of families in old barns, which are more unhealthful than tents. One family had just received the check and bought a tent and was moving to a camp. They were so glad, you'd think they had fallen heir to a ranch. In one old barn we found a poor woman with 9 children. She was big with child again, they had no stove, no covers, so they slept at night with some calves to keep them warm. The husband was out hunting work. And they were hungry. How brave they all are. I have not heard one complaint! They aren't broken and docile but they don't complain. The reason many of them have spirit is because of the way Mr. Collins has organized the camps into little functional democracies, in which they have their own government, and all take part with a central committee elected by them! (More about this when I see you.) Of course, the camps I've visited are not organized because they are all new ones, but many of the people were in other organized camps—all squatter camps. They all want work and hate to have help. We have actually had to force it on several because they would starve. No other relief worker would do this. The sight of starving doesn't affect the SERA. Many have died of starvation, but there is no way to check because the coroner lists other causes, and the files would not show whether the person was a migrant or not. But in conversation, they say here and there that their little boy died, their little girl, a husband, a mother, and so on. We were welcomed by one family because Tom Collins had arrived when they were all in bed and couldn't get up from hunger: an old man and woman, their daughter (who was very attractive), her husband, and two children. The baby was almost dead; it had cried until too weak even for that. They were all up, looking fine—isn't it amazing. They must all live entirely on starches and their skins are all clear. An excess of sweets or meat in this way would cause bad skins, but this strangely doesn't, although it certainly isn't a healthful diet.

So many poor women are pregnant, and they have their babies on newspapers, without doctors, and somehow most of them survive. Some of them die of course, more than we know. Tom Collins has even had to deliver babies—over a hundred already, and he isn't a doctor, but he says he has learned the fundamental things to do from necessity. The poor cannot afford birth control, and when there is nothing but poverty all the time, sex is the only pleasure they have.

There are 250,000 people like that in California and they represent more. Someday America will rumble with their voices against injustice and greed, someday they will rise up to a man and demand to live like decent human beings in a world they have made for others. It may be a terrible day, but a few people have made it inevitable and necessary. There will have to come a day of fighting against the darkness and cruelty of fascism, and we must make these people ready along with the people in the cities. Fascism is bringing terrific pressure to bear now on the government; they are ready in the east, and this state is already fascist. Our own government is in fear of its life, and the people are not ready to save themselves. Many of them are ready, but they need to be prepared in an orderly way. No matter how much we would like to have a peaceful life, we live in a time of history that will not permit it. I do not care to live under fascism. I'd rather die fighting to live in a free country, if there is no other way than to fight. I think the fascists will force us all to fight or submit. I am not afraid anymore to get out of my nice clothes in the city and go out in the fields with the people. There is work to do in the cities, but more people like to do it, and I feel more at home here.

One day I visited 65 families, interviewed 30 men, and walked miles, and came back feeling wonderful. Another day I walked 12 miles seeing people, and felt good. I am tired but pleasantly so, and I don't feel the nervous and irritable way I feel after a day at the office. I suppose being outdoors is good for my nerves, and that's one of my worst difficulties. Of course, if I walked that far in the city, on the pavements, smelling the gas of cars, I'd be half-dead. At the end of the first day, after seeing the people living worse than I had even imagined, I suddenly started to cry while I was eating and had to come back to my room. Once during the day I almost broke, but I had to hold myself tight against it, because they have enough troubles without that, and if we felt bad, they'd feel worse. They know we like them and want to help them without seeing our tears. When Steinbeck first came, he had to stop seeing them before the day was out. Tom Collins said he said: "By god! I can't stand anymore! I'm going away and blow the lid off this place." I think he got the man out for the pictures.

4 DUST BOWL TALES

We will be nearly finished, I think, when we stop understanding the old pull toward green things and living things, toward dirt and rain and heat and what they spawn.

JOHN GRAVES

Their early years and adolescence left lasting impressions on the literary imaginations of the Great Plains writers Willa Cather, Mari Sandoz, and Sanora Babb. Long after leaving home the three women returned to their early memories as material for their novels. Each displayed an extraordinary sensitivity to the environment—the land and its soil, weather, and visual textures. Babb's High Plains confronts ecological conditions quite different from Cather's Webster County, where the average elevation is 1,900 feet, the annual rainfall more than thirty inches, and the soil a rich prairie loess. Sandoz's upper Niobrara River region of northwestern Nebraska, called the Sandhills, is subhumid, short-grass country receiving about eighteen inches of rainfall annually and scored with deep gullies suited for grazing livestock. Baca County, Colorado, in the High Plains, rises above 3,000 feet. Its sandy loam soil receives an average annual rainfall of less than sixteen inches.[1] Ecological differences on the Great Plains embrace cultural differences as well. The people who settled the High Plains of eastern Colorado and the Oklahoma Panhandle were mainly Americans by birth, not European immigrants. The early Anglo settlers (historically a place of passage, the High Plains were hunting grounds for Native Americans) arrived some twenty years later than the original settlers in Nebraska.

Babb's landscape descriptions, like Cather's and Sandoz's, resemble a topographic map. Susan J. Rosowski justly cites the influence of the botanist Charles E. Bessey on Cather's early writing. Valorizing Sandoz's interest in the traditions and environment of her little-known Sandhills were her teachers, Louise Pound, a folklorist, and Lowry C. Wimberley, editor of the *Prairie Schooner*. Babb was influenced by Paul B. Sears and other botanists at the University of Oklahoma in the 1930s who linked the destruction of organic soil composition to improper dryland tilling in the High Plains that consumed fertility and resulted in the "dirty thirties."

The ecological disasters and economic cycles of the High Plains are associated in Babb's writings with broken dreams, human tragedies brought about by false expectations, bad science, speculative financing, and the restless demand for land. Agricultural historians tell us that farmers were negligent in their conservation practices as wheat prices fell following World War I; few had experience in dry farming techniques. Recently, Leslie Hewes has studied agricultural risk factors in the Great Plains, showing, through a study of insurance rates, that relatively low rates apply in south-central Nebraska, the setting of Cather's prairie novels, where continuous cropping occurs; and that much higher rates are assessed in Babb's Baca County in eastern Colorado, despite soil conservation programs such as summer fallow.

The cultural and social counterparts of ecological difference on the Great Plains in the novels of Cather, Sandoz, and Babb are the origins and motives of the people who settled and farmed there. The ethnic communities we know from Cather's prairie novels and Mari Sandoz's Sandhills novels are generally absent from Babb's High Plains writings. Many of Babb's people are attracted by the isolation and unbounded space of the High Plains. Some are discontented with their lives and wish to begin over. Others come wishing to lead isolated existences, and still others are drifters and losers who attach themselves to no cohesive community. "Encouraged by speculators," Nancy Burns writes in her study of the region, "many a settler of the Great Plains hoped for a quick rise in his property's value, but if things did not work, there was plenty of room to try again. They believed in a never-ending frontier" (13). Speculation and hope, yes, but the severe growing conditions on the High Plains increased the risk of loss. The inevitable consequence of high agricultural production meant fewer farmers on larger farms. This national trend afflicted the dryland farmers more than it did their prairie counterparts to the east.

Under pressure to open marginal lands, the federal government permitted homesteading on the High Plains as late as 1913. A human as well as ecological disaster was in the making. Alexandra Bergson's determination and intelligence (Cather's *O Pioneers!*) transform her farm into a prosperous enterprise. The dryland farmers of Babb's short stories and novels are ultimately thwarted; inappropriate farming practices coupled with lack of rainfall destroy the fragile ecological balance of the High Plains.

In early short stories set on the High Plains such as "Dry Summer" and "The Dark Earth," Babb portrays the whims of market forces and unforgiving nature that assail the farmers who are unable to adapt. "The Dark Earth" first appeared in a little magazine published in Beverly Hills, California, in late 1934. In 1987 she wrote a foreword to a new edition, including three additional stories, published by Capra Press with the title, *The Dark Earth & Other Stories from the Great Depression.*

THE DARK EARTH

The still heat of summer was on the land until evening when the air turned sharp with frosty cold. In the afternoon of the fourth day, Deller was going along a road that lay flat on the plains. It was more like a country walk than when he crunched along the elevated highway, his feet slipping in the white gravel. But he was tired and sore and there was no pleasure in the thought. There had been few rides. Few cars came this way. People were afraid of being held up, or perhaps they did not care if a man had no other way to travel. He could walk, he was used to walking, it was the hunger he minded.

He stopped at a farm where the house sat up porchless close to the highway in a dry yard with no grass, and walked around to the back door. A few chickens were sitting close to a shed with their eyes closed upward against the dust, and another was ruffling its feathers and wallowing about in a pile of ashes. A grimy white cloth on the clothesline was snapping in the wind. While he was waiting for someone to answer his knock, he noticed the familiar mop and dishpan hanging on the house beside the door, and on the other side of the door a warped mirror and a dirty pink comb with many teeth out above a washbasin also hanging on the house. He could hear stealthy steps and whispering inside. They were a long time coming to the door. Finally a little girl turned the knob quickly and stood in the light. She did not say anything and he smiled at her.

"Ask your mother," he said, "if I can have a little something to eat. Ask her if there is some work I can do for it." The little girl began to cry and slammed the door in panic. As he turned away he saw her and her mother pulling the curtain back a little and peering out at him. The woman dropped the curtain quickly, and he turned out of the yard with a feeling of guilt and shame.

Outside the fence he stood for a moment remembering the little girl crying, then he went on not looking back. The prairie was slowly ending. He was walking out of the unwilling level country where he belonged. Plains were cut deeply now by indistinct and smoky blue, the Rockies were rising against the edge of the sky like a dark sullen storm gathering. Even here, twenty yards to the right of him, he felt the nothingness beyond the rim of a precipice. He was coming, one step, two, three, how many in a day into a disrupted earth he did not know. A quick current of fear and curiosity flowed through him for a moment and was gone, buried in weariness. He yearned back to the flat open country he understood, and he turned his feet on the road and looked for the straight far meeting of earth and space, but already the land was rising up gently, closing him in, pressing him on to the clear wide hollows. His loneliness too and his yearning fell away with all thought and feeling into weariness. Now there was only the heaviness of his body moving, under the heat that seemed to fasten parasitic upon him in terrible concentration because his was the only movement in the still hot afternoon.

If they were wondering at home why he had come away with no word for them, he could not answer then or now. The two little girls, Lonnie and Myra, would ask questions and Cora would tell them he had gone away to work, and if they came upon her crying, she would say that he did not feel well, and the little girls would go away together knowingly, filled with a sense of mystery and tragedy around them. After awhile they might forget him, but they would remember the strangeness grown into their young hearts: they would be older with the burden of themselves he had left them to know. They would mature quickly on the mother's sorrow, and the bare knowledge of hard lean days, and time that passed now, darkly and slowly through their uncertain hands. Cora would be asking in the nights why he had gone, but in the days, she would know through patience that he could not have gone at all with words of going between them. She would cease to wonder why he had gone and begin to wait with a sureness that made him know that at length he would return. Awareness of the strange country and the monotonous walking sank away; his eyes were seeing his thoughts. On the outside there was but the automatic movement of walking; he was alive back there.

This was the year, they had said together, that luck would have to change for them; this was the last year they could meet the storms of lightning that struck the ripe crops to burning and thunder drums that shook the earth and brought no rain; the last autumn they could plant the winter wheat and wait for the snows that were too late falling; the last spring they could wheedle for seed. He had watched the wheat from the first days—they had both watched it—he and Cora. They had stood in the yard shading their eyes from the sun, looking each day to see the dark earth becoming greener with leaves urging up to the light. When the green stems were certain and cool to the touch, they had walked on Sundays through the field, plucking stray weeds and carrying them away in their pockets lest they take root and live where they had fallen. Weeds were always stronger than the man-planted seeds. He would dig his hands into the earth to know how near the surface moisture came, or kick the clods to see them part quickly into dry dust or scatter dark and clinging with dampness. The wheat came up to their knees, strong and thick, the heads were swollen fat, closed in their green sheaths, soon to burst to the sun. They were not full-grained, but they were growing into the summer months. A few heavy snows had given the wheat a good start, the spring had gone by with little rain, and the summer was dry and hot. Warm strong winds blew over the land, picking up the dry surface of earth, beating lightly against the houses and crops. Now when he walked through the wheat he found blades yellowing and drooping, but most of the grain stood up against the sun and the wind, growing taller, losing its tender greenness, ready to spring into ripeness. There would be a crop without rain, a better crop if it had rained, but a crop without rain. He began to recall the last years' prices. They had been so low a farmer could not live. Let's see, three hundred twenty acres, a small farm, he ought to get another half section to wheat next year. He would do well to get five or six bushels to the acre a dry year like this; a wet year he might have had thirty or forty. A dollar a bushel in good times, well, sixty-five or seventy cents now, maybe fifty. Three hundred-twenty times six, one thousand nine hundred and twenty bushels, seventy cents, one thousand three hundred and forty-four dollars. He thought of the expenses.

The wheat came up around his legs golden ripe, the beards were prickly and dry. Every day now he walked through the field, watching for the last of the greenness, waiting for the final ripeness. Every day more of the wheat was curling and drooping under the heat and dust. The strips that were still green were not ripening—they were bending weakly, burned and dying. When the wind came through the field, he could hear above the swaying ripe sound, the crackle of the dead wheat. Maybe he could not hear it but the sound was in his ears from somewhere. He could hear the machines humming on other fields miles away. He had reckoned the time for harvest within a week, and he was right. There would be a crop, a smaller crop, but the grain standing was fair wheat.

The partly cut field lay like a geometric design against the open land around it; the uncut wheat stood up sharply in a straight line away from the bristling path of stubble. The crew of harvesters made loud jokes about beating the hail, and looked doubtfully into the sky like superstitious men knocking on wood to make their words good. At the house, Cora cooked and washed dishes from morning till night, and served to the hungry men food bought on time, on the strength of their crop. There was not room in the house for the men, and the heat from the stove made the kitchen no retreat from the sun. An old table had been set up in the yard and Lonnie and Myra carried the dishes back and forth, and kept the flies away from the food by waving flour-sack towels. There were no trees; only a few of the older, more prosperous farms had trees. The men sat in the hard bare yard under the glaring shadowless noon, eating, then resting and smoking awhile before going back into the field. By evening meal time, cool had come over the land, bringing faint odors of weeds and grass and the dark earth, and the full ripe breath of wheat.

The next day, with only part of the crop combined, a brown wall had mounted and hung over half the sky from morning till late afternoon. It lay back upon the northwest, opaque, sullen, an awful suspended strength. The air was hot and ominously still. The men worked in a kind of resignation and frenzy. They had ceased to speak of the loss of the wheat. They watched the heavy cloud, waiting like animals to escape when it would descend. But they worked, no one speaking out in fear, wishing to stop. The wheat was waiting brightly yellow, rippling faintly now and then with the smallest breath of wind, the wave flowing over its surface from one edge to another. Then as if all life around them were interrupted, without breath, there was a sudden, sinister lull everywhere. Space was a vacuum. An intense waiting was in the air. Nothing stirred and the great dark wall was everything, the silence was everything. The sound of the combine stopped as the quiet came and the men drew swiftly into a loose group, walking quickly, beginning to run toward the house, into the cellar under the house. No one saw that Deller did not leave, but moved wordlessly behind the machine where he could not be seen, where he could watch the storm until it broke. Almost slyly a cool damp wind came into the lifeless air, and was lost in the sudden roar that followed. The great cloud sprang out at them all, loosed in a booming fury of straight wind, filled with dust, so that nothing could be seen even a foot away. He dropped down to the earth and gripped the wheel of the tractor that he was sure could not be moved. The men had reached the house. Cora and the little girls had gone into the cellar before them. He lay there with the terrible sound in his ears, feeling the dust cutting into him like little spears of stone. He heard the cracking of an idle header and the sound of its flight across the field. The tractor quivered but held its place.

When he stood up, the wind was blowing hard and cold, thick with dust. He could see the house dimly standing, unharmed. The wheat was lying flat to the earth, combed in smoothness toward him, broken and useless. Layers of dirt were lying over parts of it, and the wheels of the machine were half buried in the fine dry dust. He looked at the devastation a long time, wiping the dirt from his face and out of his ears, and slapping his overalls and shirt. Then he turned away from his field and walked toward the main road. He saw the coat he had worn in the cool morning blown from the machine flat against the fence like a scarecrow. The air was still heavy with dust and they could not see from the house. Large scattered drops of rain fell into the stifling air. The wind turned colder. The rain hardened into ice points and pierced and stung his face. The drought broke in a great rush of sound—the loose breaking he knew so well. With an ultimate bursting forth the round white hailstones fell on the ground, springing and rolling about in a dance. He walked over the stubble, numbly aware that he was beaten and chilled by the hail. It turned again into rain, and the rain fell scantily, as if wishing to stop. He looked up to the thick ragged clouds separating swiftly, the rain "going over." The dust would probably blow again tomorrow.

He cursed the dry lands, he cursed himself for being a farmer, but he wanted only to cry out brokenly against the infinity that lay like an enemy beyond his grasp, beyond his understanding. He wanted to cry out for help to the great nothingness that had no ears for his tragedy. He wanted to ask the immensity around him: the wind, the fallen sky, the earth: to give him back his crop: his faith. And knowing how pitiful and lost his prayer, he went on locked in his suffering, inarticulate, despairing. He did not know why he was turning away from his ruined fields. He was a man who had worked the earth and knew no other way of living. He had given no time to weeping and asking: the days had been full and hard, and the nights darkly unknown with sleep. By the time he had reached the highway, he was saying surely to himself, "A man can work at something else—a man can always get a job if he tries hard enough!" He looked at the fields of others along the road buried under the thick dust. Wash tubs and buckets, light implements, chicken coops, and sheds were strewn over the land. White Leghorn chickens with all their feathers blown backwards were lying dead along the road. Cows and horses were standing in the pastures with their behinds to the storm, their heads lowered, waiting. Any job would beat farming. He would send them enough money to get through the winter. Maybe the next year would be a good one if there were enough snow. No, any job . . . they would move to town.

By long stretches of walking and short rides he had come over, the prairies of western Kansas, eastern Colorado, into mountainous western Colorado. Outside of Pretty Prairie, he had worked two days on a farm where one of the hands had been overcome by heat. He asked for work at every farm he passed, but there was nothing. In the towns, he was hesitant, wondering what jobs he could do and where to find them. He went to the creameries where they sold poultry, to the feed stores and the draymen, and finally to anyone. The answer was always the same: hard times, no jobs, and when there were jobs they must go to local men. He was told by others like himself to keep moving, he might be picked up for vagrancy. When he got to Denver he learned about soup kitchens and flop houses, and he heard about the opening of a silver mine in New Mexico. He did not write to his wife because he had no money. But on the way out of Denver a young girl gave him a quarter at a door where he asked for food. She went away for a moment and came back with the coin, smiling widely to cover her sympathy. "I hope this will help a little," she said, and the quarter in his hand felt like a dollar. He bought a stamped envelope, wrote a few words on a money-order blank, wrapped a dime in another blank and mailed it to his wife. He said he was on his way to the silver mines where he could get a job.

He caught a ride into Jolla, New Mexico, too tired and hungry to look any more with wonder on the great hard mountains and the colored rocks. His feet were sore, and his bones ached from sleeping out in the cold nights. The Mexicans and their quick broken speech filling the streets with sound were strange to him. He walked about watching for the lighter faces of his kind, but they were stranger than the others. He followed some men into a saloon. There was gambling in the back and one of the gamblers saw him standing around and asked him when he had eaten last. Everybody called him "Easy" because he was big-hearted with the down-and-outers. "Easy" was talking to him about the drought in the wheat belt, and told him to wait around until he was through work. They went out to eat and Deller asked him about the silver boom.

"Man, I hope you didn't come out here for that!" and "Easy" shook his head at Deller. "No good," he said. "A little new mining, but these places are dead. You a miner too?"

"No, I just want to work."

"It's no good here, no money, no work for outsiders." They ate without talking, Deller thinking about the silver mines. The other man could sense his disappointment.

"If you want to get to the silver mines, why don't you go to Nevada? Catch a ride to Reno; you can get out there for Juneville. That's where the great Wilstock lode is, if you want to do some mining. Know anything about it?"

"Not much," he said.

"Well, you can roust about for awhile, make a little money. Hang around here a few days with me and maybe get you a ride up that way. I live here at a cabin camp; you'll have a place to sleep."

When Deller got a ride north toward the end of the week, the gambler gave him a few dollars, and a straw hat. He was almost a week getting to Juneville there were so few rides. He would walk only to the edge of the little sun-baked towns and wait on the highway. A man has to be careful about walking through the desert. The towns are far apart and there is no water between them. His shoes were worn through in places and his feet were sore. His hair was too long and his clothes were dirty, but the activity in Juneville aroused a little of the old hope. Men were moving about; they talked easily; he learned the mining terms and used them. He stood about for hours watching the ore come to the surface in the little tramcars, shoved to the end of the tipple and dumped into the chutes that lead to the ore bins. From the bins, he learned, it reached the stamp mill and then the reduction works, and he marveled at it all. He looked at the great hard mountains from which the silver ore was taken, and his thoughts leapt on to the silver coins at the end. He got a job as a mucker, and sent Cora what he could spare of his pay, without a letter. He was too much ashamed to write and he was afraid to know the reply. He read in the papers that others had thrown away how the dust was blowing in the middlewest, how the rivers and streams were drying up and the cattle and horses were dying for want of water and grass. Every day he was thinking of his farm, and Cora and the little girls, but at nights when he might have written, his thoughts fell away under a wearied aching sleep, helpless before the heaviness of his body drugged with the daylight's hard labor. Juneville was the hottest place he had ever been, but down three thousand feet into the earth, the heat was almost more than the miners could endure.

As suddenly as his job had come, it was taken away: there were better muckers than Deller, the town was full of them. But he had got a job once and he might get another so he stayed on, making the rounds, hoping with a strange hopelessness and despair, and finally not even despair but a quiet insensibility to the answers when he asked for work. His money was gone. He slept about with others like himself in any shelter he could find, and tried to beg ten or fifteen cents a day for food. He would have stayed on, no longer wondering what else to do, but he kept reading the papers about the drought, and he had to get home.

He put new cardboard in his shoes and started walking down the long narrow mountain ways to Reno. He waited around Reno for a ride into Colorado, but finally started hitchhiking to Salt Lake City. He had never ridden the rods of a train and had not quite the courage to try, but in Salt Lake City he could get a freight through to Colorado and he went. In Colorado he could feel the sharp coolness of autumn in the air, and he thought vaguely of the winter, not knowing how it could be met. East of the Rockies the land stretched away into the lonely, sparsely settled plains with their long straight roads pointing into the horizon as far as the eye could see. The heat quickened on the lowlands, and a fine powdery dust drifted over the prairies on the hot wind. He saw now that many of the crops had not been harvested at all. Wheat lay flat on the ground half buried in the dry brown powder. On some of these farms the houses looked empty and deserted. There were no chickens in the yards and no sounds of life. When he saw any cattle they were standing inert or lying about dozing with weakness. Their bones stood out strongly under their lusterless hides. He passed a large stock tank in a pasture where the cattle moved restlessly about it, bawling and waiting. A few row crops stretched away from the highway stunted and dried before they had reached maturity. Their leaves rustled like paper in the wind.

When he came into the country where his farm lay, it was the same: the dried crops, the buried wheat, the starving cattle eating the dusty dried buffalo grass they had already cropped into the earth, the heat and the wind and the dust, everywhere. He saw his house and barn, two indefinite specks in the distance, swimming in a mirage, the shimmering water of a mirage, and he went on without any change of feeling, knowing what he must find there. When he was a mile away, he left the highway and walked across the field where his wheat had fallen under the cloud of dust the months before. The loose sifted dirt came into the open soles of his shoes but his feet were toughened until there was no feeling of the earth. The house stood gaunt and alone in the flat yard ahead of him, and when he saw through the house from one curtainless window to another, he knew they had gone. He went on, feeling no surprise. The kitchen door was open a little way and he went inside. Some of the things were there, but the rooms were bare of curtains and quilts and clothes that had given them life. The haunted uncovered windows gaped into all the world outside; the lonely house surrounded him mutely, remindful and lost. He saw that they had not been gone long, and he stood at a window wondering where they could be. They were not far, he knew, because they had no place to go, and he went outside to look at the farms nearest, to look for signs of life on them. He saw how the dust had drifted like snow high against one side of the house and covered the machinery in the yard. Toward the north lay a farm a half mile away on the opposite side of the road; the others were five and eight miles to the south and east. Everywhere lay devastation, the coating of dust over the grass and crops, but the wind had settled into a cool slow current. He saw a woman taking clothes from the line at the farm to the north and he knew it was Cora. He stood a long while watching her piling the white things onto her arm and moving slowly along the line. He looked about the yard for the little girls but they were nowhere in sight. The owner's wife was bending over something in the yard. Cora was facing him but she was busy with the clothes. He climbed upon the seat of a harrow standing in the yard and waved and waved at the woman a half-mile away. She kept on with her work. He took his shirt off then and waved it back and forth slowly when he thought she was looking. Finally he saw one of the little girls dart out of the farmyard, then the other, and the mother hurry into the house. The little girls came out upon the main road running toward the farm. He jumped down from the harrow seat, forgetting his ravaged strength, and ran out of the farmyard into the highway. He saw Cora walking, hurrying, along the road ahead. The little girls met him first and they looked strangely at his ragged clothes and the whiskers on his face, but they clung to his hands and danced along the road to meet their mother. They had discovered him, it was their triumph. He saw the age and the pain in Cora's face, and she saw the defeat in him, and she smiled a little. When she was near enough to make him hear, she said, "Well!" and began to run toward him.

—*The Magazine* (Nov.–Dec. 1934)

Sanora published an excerpt from an early version of her unpublished first novel, "Whose Names Are Unknown," in the *Kansas Magazine* (1941). The cruel realities of migrant farm labor appear in this short story drawn from her work experiences in the FSA camps. Tom Collins, whom Sanora assisted in the FSA camps, is "Woody." Here Babb shows the slow rise to consciousness among the refugee farmers and their determination to resist the forces that are strangling them.

MORNING IN IMPERIAL VALLEY

The next morning early Milt went to the Office tent and knocked. There was no answer and he walked away looking around the camp. He saw one of the camp guards and inquired. The young man pointed to a low tent pitched soft on the ground without sideboards.

"He's in there. Just go over and knock on the tent pole if you're in a hurry."

Milt hesitated and thought of waiting, then walked over. They were all hungry; they couldn't wait any longer.

As he neared the tent he heard queer smothered sounds within, stifled breath coming quick and hard. He stood there listening, wanting to go away, but he kept thinking of Lonnie who stayed in bed because she was too weak to get up. He heard a man's voice, low, and another man in answer. He knocked on the pole. A man about thirty-five with a scared, tense face pushed back the flap. He said nothing, just looked.

"Is Mr. Woody here?" Milt asked.

"He's here," the man said. "Come in." As Milt stepped in, the man turned as if he had not meant to say what he had, and spoke nervously. "You mind to see him?" Woody turned and looked at Milt.

"Good morning," he said, and seeing Milt going out, he added: "Wait. You can give us a hand."

Confused by the muffled sounds from the corner, and the conflicting words, Milt came back into the tent, feeling uncomfortable. The air was close. Under his feet the dirt was powdered deep. As his eyes accustomed themselves to the half-light, he looked toward the corner Woody and the man were watching, and he saw a woman lying on the ground, with only a battered mattress between her and the dirt. Her face was tight with strain and her breath came hard. Now and then she groaned and whimpered a little. The ragged quilt swelled over her body. On the stove a bucket of water steamed. He looked at the woman again.

"Maybe they'd take me in the hospital now—maybe, if we could go now—while I'm like this," she pleaded. "It's so dirty here, *I'm afraid*." The sweat ran down her face, making it shine in the dusky room.

"They won't take you, honey," her husband said. "Mr. Woody here's sent out, tryin' to get one of the state nurses. Don't worry none, just quiet

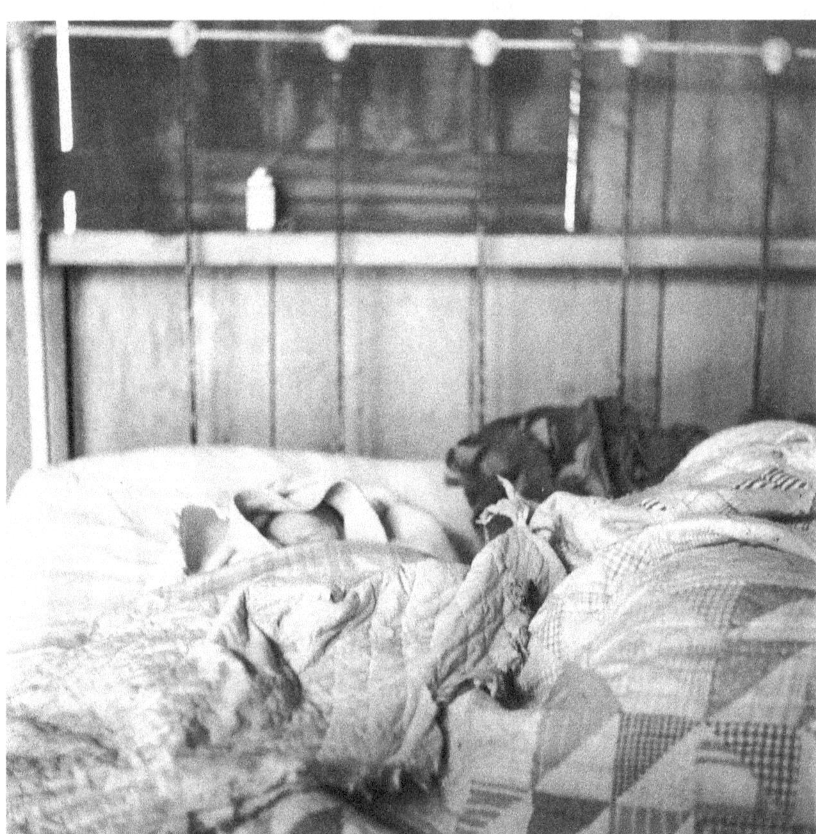

Sick child

Clinic in Hanford, California

yourself." The woman looked at him, and for a few moments she was quieter, trying not to show her pain.

"Donne," Woody said, "could one of the women come over and help? Ask one of them to bring some clean rags, and if she hasn't any, have her ask in the other tents. See if you can find some newspapers. We haven't much time."

Milt was glad to escape the heated tent, glad to have something to do. He forgot his hunger and that of the children seeing the woman lying in the dark corner, under the sloping oily wall of the tent. He hurried to his tent and told Julia, then to their old Kansas neighbor, Mrs. Starbuck, and after showing them where to go, he went in search of newspapers. In a little while the whole camp had come alive, and women were rushing about, speaking to neighbors they had not known before, finding rags, asking for baby clothes. Milt came back with an armful of old newspapers and handed them through the flap to Woody. He could hear them spreading the papers on the bed. Mrs. Starbuck handed out a small pail.

"Get me some water. I'm gonna sprinkle down this floor."

The woman was quiet for a long time; then her groans came loud and strong. A knot of people stood in front of the tent ready to run for needs. Tortured cries ripped the air and stopped, leaving a silence filled with awe, to be rent again and again.

"Oh, please God, get me a doctor!" the woman screamed. Voices came out of the tent, gentle, soothing.

"We're right here. Everything will be all right."

"Try hard now. It won't be long." Screams slashed across the voices.

"Please! Can't somebody bring me a doctor!" Her voice subsided for a moment. "Maybe an aspirin. Hasn't anybody got an aspirin tablet?"

She groaned. There was quick movement in the tent. She groaned heavily, then sharply, then her voice came screaming frenzy. It rose and rose, cold, horrible, louder: "I have to suffer like this because we're poor, that's why, only poor! *They* don't have babies without doctors, starved babies they don't want! Where is God's Wrath? It only falls on us! Even God is on their side! Do you hear—*even* God!"

"Sh-h-h, Virgie, sh-h-h" they could hear her husband saying.

"I'm not afraid," she cried in anguish. "*Even God!* Hear it, God. You can all keep on prayin'. But I'll die *hatin'—hatin' somethin' out there that keeps us from earnin' our bread!* Keeps me from havin' a doctor. I don't wanta live no more like this! I wanta die! God let me—" A shrill scream of pain cut her breath and when it was over she groaned with weariness, and was quiet.

The agonized hours dragged on, her weak voice whimpered faintly, then not at all. They stood outside until it was all over, looking at one another, shaking their heads when there was a tormented sound of life. Milt felt helpless.

"That poor Woody's had to deliver a lot of farm workers' babies when they can't get a doctor! If we ain't citizens a this state we ain't nothin' by their way a thinkin'," an old man said.

They heard a baby cry, weak and thin, and they all stood quiet, waiting. Mrs. Starbuck came out of the tent for a moment fanning herself.

"How is she?" they asked at once. "Is she—?"

"That poor critter's too weak to move," Mrs. Starbuck said, wiping the sweat off her face with her apron. "When a woman don't eat, it's time agin as hard for her. Her knees got up and they wouldn't come down. It was terrible!"

"Is the baby—?" a woman asked timidly. Mrs. Starbuck interrupted her, her face reddening with anger and her voice trembling.

"That baby looks like a little old man, and not a pound of good solid flesh on him. It ain't his fault he comes in the world, and then he comes in starved. It's shameful!" She turned abruptly and went into the tent. The people muttered quietly and waited. Mrs. Starbuck came out again in a flurry.

"The poor soul's got no milk for the baby! Reckon any women in camp nursing babies could nurse him a little and keep him alive till we get hold of some milk? He's all dried up—even his tongue is dry." One of the women came up carrying some clean but worn baby clothes and handed them to Mrs. Starbuck.

"I'm Mrs. King," she said. "I'm on the women's committee. We can see about it and try to get some fresh milk tomorrow."

"Fresh milk?" a woman asked. "That costs money. None of the kids have fresh milk!"

"Well, we have to find *some* way," Mrs. King said. She and three other women spoke together, separated and went their ways. One of them got in a car and drove off toward Calipatria.

"There she goes," a man said, shading his eyes from the blinding morning sun, as he watched after the noisy car. "They been savin' that gas a long time to drive to the field with first day a work."

"Anybody in camp got any meat, I wonder?" another man asked.

"He's havin' a little pipe dream," someone said, and they laughed quietly.

"Well, now, I was just wonderin'. Thought if we could find a bite we could make a little broth for the woman in there, give her some strength." Milt listened quietly to these new neighbors.

"I got no meat, but I'll fix her somethin' hot after a bit," a woman said. "She ain't thinkin' about eatin' now."

The tent flap was pushed open, and Milt saw his wife come out, pale and tired. Her hair was damp and sticking to her forehead.

"She's asleep," Julia said, smiling weakly, and walked toward their tent. Woody came out next, carrying a hammock of blood-stained rags. One of the men went forward to help him.

"We'll go out in the clearing and burn these," Woody said.

"We'll take 'em," the man said. "You'd better rest." Woody looked worn out and sick.

"One of these days I'll get arrested for practicing without a license," he said smiling at them as he walked off toward his office.

"Nobody else to do it," a woman said, and after he was out of hearing, "None these other 'fficial men *would* do it either." She poked her head in the tent. "I'll sit with her awhile now. You get some rest." After awhile Mrs. Starbuck came out.

"Where's *he*?" a man asked.

"He's sittin' on a box sound asleep," she said. "I never saw a husban' stay around like that. He felt sick and I told him to come out in the air, but he was afraid somethin' should happen to her." She lowered her voice to a whisper. "It may too. We've got to take care. She was brave all right, but sometimes it takes more'n courage." She sighed wearily, and started away. "Lordy! Lordy! I got to see about my kids." The other woman went in and before Mrs. Starbuck had got far, she came out, looking glum, her mouth in a tight angry line.

"That baby won't need no milk," she said.

— *Kansas Magazine* (1941)

Babb poured personal experience and observation, recorded in her field notes, reportage, and short stories, into the novel *Whose Names Are Unknown*. It stands as the capstone of her understanding of fundamental social and political forces that change people's lives, sometimes in abrupt and cruel ways. The focus of her novel is the intimacy of family life under great duress.[2] Her purpose was not to publicize the refugees' plight so much as to give voice to the voiceless, to tell the stories that the refugees might have written had they the time and ability to do so. We enter their lives; there is little mediation on the author's part. Babb traces the slow but credible growth of political consciousness in a people who are by instinct independent, self-reliant, and conservative. Their uprooting and migration are tragic interludes; their aspirations are to resume their lives as independent farmers.

One of a generation of literary radicals, Babb did not however structure *Whose Names Are Unknown* as a proletarian conversion or a strike novel. She knew her dryland farmers too well. She honored them as individual people, not as symbolic figures bearing the sociohistorical burden of a failed economy and natural catastrophe. The problem with realism is that it ages more quickly than does parable—language, manners, attitudes attach more firmly to the time in which the work was written. Yet a work of radical vision written some sixty years ago still has value in reinscribing history into present-day contexts, linking the dispossession of the dryland farmers with uprooting and displacement everywhere and at any time. Babb's first novel prefigures ecofeminist concerns today in its circular narrativity and intimacy, its connectedness in place of binary "we-they" relations with others and with nature.[3]

WHOSE NAMES ARE UNKNOWN (EXCERPT)

In spite of the time of year, the sun beat down hotly on their stooping backs, and the cotton sack dragged up a thin dust from the ground and the drying plants, which were already stubborn and catchy to walk through. Autumn comes gently in the easy semi-tropical climate, with none of the pungent smells or decaying leaves or the sharp fragrance of a changing year. Seasons slip from one to the other with scarcely a natural sign. The landscape is always green, with here and there a grove of deciduous trees leafing and shedding bare according to their temperate habit. The midwesterners knew the month and the crop of every valley, and they knew that the mountains were green in winter and brown in summer, and they marveled at the fabulous land sheltered from the violences of nature they had fought at home.

Milt moved steadily along the leafy aisle, picking with precision and speed, his eye on the next boll before his hand left another. He knew every way to save his strength, every move to cut short the time, and yet if he stood up a moment, his back would break like a green bough toughly refusing. His shirt was wet, and the cotton strap, which Julia had padded to keep from blistering, was rubbing the sweat in a stinging hot band on his shoulder and back. Julia was picking a few rows over, ten yards behind him. He could not see Mrs. Starwood but she picked like a man, weighing in with the best of them. Frieda, like Julia, picked around one seventy-five, but there were hard days when they weighed in two hundred, and joked tiredly at supper about their speed. A tall Negro worked alongside Milt keeping the same pace. Someone worked close behind him on the other. Two rows over, keeping up with them, but leaving cotton if he fell behind, was Seff, whom they all suspected of being a stool. He tried to talk to the men and women next to him but the warning had gone round and no one exchanged more than civilities about the weather, careful then not to sound as if complaining. Sometimes he worked as if his thoughts were far away, but they knew he was listening for any chance word he could take to the boss when the day was over.

The man close behind Milt worked up even and wanted to talk. You could always tell when a man was trying to act natural.

"Whaddya say, Dunne?"

"Not much. Hot day." Milt knew his face, but could not remember his name.

"Yow. Ain't no changes a year in this country. A man don't feel right." The man suited his speed to Dunne's.

"What'd you say your name is?" Milt asked.

"Snow." He spoke lower when he gave his name. Milt looked up at him, and Snow made a slight gesture with his head and his eyes toward Seff. Milt glanced at the Negro beside him, and the Negro nodded his head once downward and kept on picking. Milt picked a while without talking.

"Whaddya think of the seventy-five?" Snow asked.

"Can't make much at it," Milt said, not looking up.

"Either of you hear the fellas talking?"

"Powerful lot of talking over'n that end of the field," the Negro said.

"What's your name?" Milt asked him. "Mine's Dunne."

"Garrison."

Milt waited automatically to hear the "suh" and when it did not come, he was relieved. He had been wondering how he would say it, tell him not to. We're both pickin' cotton for the same hand-to-mouth wages. I'm no better'n he is; he's no worse. The memory of being called a white nigger in Imperial Valley lay in his mind unforgotten, sore, like an exposed nerve. Milt looked at him. Garrison looked back, his eyes straight, and there was no difference.

"Man, don't be talking too much 'round here. I worked here for three years. I know 'em."

"You're not in camp?" Milt asked.

"No-o," Garrison said smiling in a way that Milt did not understand. "We got a camp our own three miles away."

Milt understood the implication, but he dared not voice his sympathy in the face of this man's dignity.

"Say," Snow said, still in a low voice, "there's a lot of talk in the field. The men are getting sore as hell about the light bill and no cash till Saturday and then like as not they don't draw nothing. And the seventy-five. Whaddya think?"

"What do you figger we think?" Garrison asked.

"What's it matter what we think?" Milt asked.

"That's just it. I ain't just asking fool's questions looking for fool's answers." Snow stopped and picked silently for some time. "That sonofabitch cocking his ear over there. You'll get yours, buddy, ain't room enough in this man's world for a skunk that shaves. Whyn't you get a little ambition and go be a pimp?" Snow was talking to himself.

Garrison smiled. "He gets het up."

"Well, as I was saying," Snow went on sarcastically, "the men were talking about setting down around the field some morning. All setting around so's they can't bring nobody else in. It's as easy as rolling off a log, if we all do it. We'll set there till we get ninety cents or a dollar."

"Jus' as e-easy as rollin' off a log," Garrison drawled.

"Well, why not?" Snow demanded, picking fast.

"Not so loud," Milt said.

"Who'll take charge and kind of lead us 'case things don't go right?" Garrison asked, very low.

"Any of us. If we all set down we don't need to worry about no leader. It'll be over before your ass gets tired."

"He's long on strong talk," Garrison said to Milt.

"How many will do it when the time comes?" Milt asked.

"Ain't a man here satisfied with being robbed of his labor," Garrison said. "But most of 'em'll be afraid, and you can't blame 'em. Got to be *somebody* responsible. These poor men and women ain't gonna foller a lot of wind." Milt felt himself drawn to the logic of the Negro, and still, the other fellow was right: if they *all* sat down, they'd get more like what was coming to them, and it wouldn't take long. Day after tomorrow he might be making \$2.70 or even \$3.00 instead of the top \$2.25.

"What do you say, Dunne? Old Professor over there, he's gonna hold out for a captain with brass buttons."

"Not that," Garrison said unperturbed.

"Well," Milt said, feeling confused, "I'd sit down if the rest of 'em will."

"You gotta say yes or no; we want to know, so's we can figger."

"Who's we?" asked Garrison, never forgetting to keep his voice low.

"Just some of us fellas. We was all talking nearly ever' night, and finally we agreed to find out which way the wind blows with the rest of you."

"These people ain't letting it go so easy, I'm tellin' you," Garrison said. "We oughta be prepared. I ain't agreeing without we have somebody to advise us. I need this job powerful bad."

"Okay, Professor. We'll set down without you." Milt looked at Garrison and saw that his face was serious, worried. The Negro glanced sidewise at Milt and shook his head slowly, then he went on down the row picking with deft quick moves, hardly looking at the cotton. When he was ahead of him, it seemed to Milt that he could guess by the tired stoop of his burdened shoulders that he was disappointed in him. He felt sorry. Somehow he wanted this man's respect, and suddenly he was not ashamed to acknowledge it to himself.

—*Whose Names Are Unknown* (University of Oklahoma Press, 2004)

5 THE DUST BOWL AS SITE OF MEMORY

You know when the finance folks and the weather both set in on you at the same time, they ain't nothin' else to do but desert the farm.

WOODY GUTHRIE

Drought is a natural and frequent event on the High Plains. Yet it was not until the droughts of the 1930s that the region attracted the nation's attention. The Depression situated the droughts in a human tragedy of broad political dimensions whose tableaus of dispossession and migration lodged deep in the public consciousness. The consequences stretched well beyond the afflicted region; the Dust Bowl catastrophe focused the nation on deeply rooted political and cultural questions having to do with traditional notions of success and failure in a society that customarily counts failure as a risk one must absorb in pursuing success. The timing of the droughts coincided with a financial earthquake that intensified political debates and put in question the very institutions and beliefs that, some argued, had led to the crisis—and therefore deserved to be replaced by a new ethos and other forms of governance.

Great civilizations have collapsed over time for failing to respond sensibly to environmental change. This was the case during the period known as the Classic Maya Collapse (800–1000 C.E.). Drought brought death to millions of Maya and initiated a series of internal failures that ultimately brought down their civilization.[1] Radical environmental and human neglect has caused civilizations to perish, as Shelley's "Ozymandias" crumbled, a futile memorial to pride and folly.

The American Southwest, including Texas, lies at 30 degrees north latitude in a belt that encompasses the major deserts of the earth, including the Chihuahua and Sahara. There is little immediate prospect that the periodic cycles of drought, such as occurred in the 1890s, 1930s, 1950s, and 1990s, will bring down another civilization. Yet in the American Southwest people must learn to live within the limits imposed by increasing population and exhaustible water supplies—or face even greater crises than those that afflicted the dryland farmers.

Today California's San Joaquin Valley is a vast irrigated desert laced with water wells and canals, where multinational production and service companies supply an oil-thirsty nation's needs. Brown smog hangs over the valley, causing sickness and obscuring distant mountains. Large numbers of Mexican agricultural workers have settled in the small towns whose names were once familiar to field workers from the Great Plains and the South. In communities once largely Anglo, Latinos hold elected offices and own small businesses. The new immigrants have revived dusty hamlets in which Spanish is now the first language. The low wages and long hours of field labor, however, have not changed. Most of the new families are poor, raising concerns that immigration has simply moved the social and economic problems of Mexican villages to California towns, which lack adequate resources to deal with them. Yet most of the new immigrants claim that they would rather be poor in Porterville than in San Luis Potosí. Few children of Mexican immigrants who have settled in the United States take up the work of their parents, preferring to pursue educational opportunities in order to enter better-paying occupations.[2]

In predominantly Anglo towns such as Fresno, Visalia, and Bakersfield, the music, values, religious beliefs, and politics that the Dust Bowl migrants brought with them endure. Nearly half of the valley's three million residents, it is estimated, claim ancestors among the Dust Bowl refugees. Yet, according to Dan Morgan, "[o]nly a tiny percentage of people who migrated to California in the 1930s—an estimated 6 percent—came from the six western panhandle counties hardest hit by the Dust Bowl. Most came from the Cotton Belt of northern Texas and central and eastern Oklahoma. . . . Many of the Oklahomans who pulled up stakes in the 1930s were not even farmers" (156). Nonetheless, the values of the Dust Bowl farmers seem dominant. With few exceptions, their aim was to take root and build a new existence. Many from the Dust Bowl states brought the idioms of southwestern populism with them: a resistance to power and authoritarian government; suspicion of banks and corporate ownership, and of government. The dignity of hard work and "right living" continues to be preached in their churches and displayed on at least one billboard near Bakersfield: "Tough times come and go. Tough people are here to stay."

For the dryland farmers the family unit was a secure anchor as well as a spur to resettle and begin a new existence intact. Yet personal conflicts and divisive social forces renewed once the farmers resettled. At the center of debates today is the issue raised by natural disasters such as drought and water resources. If drought and water supplies are beyond individuals' control and constitute a threat to the social order, then government or some institution must assume responsibility for the consequences. So runs one argument. Another assigns the responsibility to local initiative without government aid. It is sufficient, according to this argument, that government assure security and justice. Both arguments turn on the fact that water rights and distribution for agricultural purposes in the Central Valley are largely controlled by large landowners and farm corporations, such as the Boswell "empire."[3]

In the old government camp of Weedpatch only one tin building and a small wooden shed that once served as the post office remain. Now called the Sunset Migrant Farm Labor Camp, it houses Mexican American families who along with other Latinos living nearby participate in the annual Dust Bowl Festival. Tamales are served along with beef barbecue, but the two communities, Anglo and Latino, rarely mix except in the schools. Prejudices once directed toward by the Okies are now attached to the new Latino immigrants. Yet aspirations for a better future and memories of hardships past serve to knit people together as fellow human beings. Drought and economic failure respect no borders. Mobility and migration create the conditions for cultural and political exchange and transformation in which place is no longer a defining element but rather sites of communication, the transmission and creation of new ideas and modes of living.

In celebrating the past through events like the Dust Bowl Festival the old-timers celebrate an era when self-reliance was a virtue and individual resourcefulness a condition for survival. In some small towns of the western valleys and the Great Plains, however, changes in land use and technological developments are bringing dramatic change to near-moribund communities. There are efforts to return the range to native grasslands by removing cattle and sheep. Organizations such as the Nature Conservancy are buying ranchland in Montana to protect against urban development.[4] In small towns where grain elevators and cotton gins once rose above the flat landscape, microwave towers and curtain-glass buildings mark the horizon. Communication and information technology are generating a new economy and influencing community values. In this new frontier of fiber optics, data compression, and software development, specialized learning and willingness to move as the sites shift are required. Relocation and changing occupational demands demand that workers adapt to unfamiliar living patterns. The looming threat of job loss, obsolescence, and outsourcing cuts deep into traditional forms of social organization. Individual resilience may still be a workable virtue, but the centrality of the family unit and the Jeffersonian ideal of self-reliance, indeed, the values of community life enshrined in the memory of the Dust Bowl refugees, are struggling to survive in the face of realities variously termed globalization, late capitalism, "the new world order"—or simply progress.

Sanora Babb witnessed these changes and recorded them in documentary reports and literature. As novelist and poet, she gave expression to the Dust Bowl farmers' aspirations, failed dreams, and struggle for dignity. She shared their aspirations and chronicled their dispossession in reportage, short story, and the novel *Whose Names Are Unknown*, whose own publication history involves blighted aspirations, endurance, and survival—a *dédoublement* of the Dust Bowl experience.

Active with the League of American Writers, Babb edited its West Coast journal *The Clipper* in the early 1940s and its successor, *The California Quarterly* (CQ), a decade later. The CQ introduced readers to the work of B. Traven, French surrealist poets, Mexican muralists, promising young writers such as Ray Bradbury and Don Gordon, and more experienced writers such as Nelson Algren, Thomas McGrath, and E. P. Thompson. Babb's connections with the cultural left threatened (by association) to jeopardize the career of her husband, the famed Chinese American cinematographer James Wong Howe. Because of California's miscegenation law forbidding intermarriage between Anglos and Chinese, even Chinese Americans, Babb and Howe were not permitted to marry until 1948, when the law was repealed.

Seeking to protect Howe from further harassment and blacklisting, Babb moved to Mexico City during the early years of the House Un-American Activities Committee hearings. There Sanora wrote short stories about the impoverished workers she had come to know in villages and Mexico City streets. Among her new friends were B. Traven (*The Treasure of the Sierra Madre*), Diego Rivera, and Waldeen (née Waldeen Falkenstein), founder of Mexico's Ballet de Bellas Artes. Her marriage to Howe, who twice won an Oscar (*The Rose Tattoo, Hud*), brought Babb into contact with the Hollywood film world. On her return to the

Refugee farmers at play, Arvin FSA camp

"They would rise and fall and, in their falling, rise again." From Sanora Babb, Whose Names Are Unknown

United States in 1951, however, she kept apart from a fast-track life, continuing to publish widely and enjoying growing recognition for her work. After two of her stories appeared in Martha Foley's *Best American Short Stories,* she was invited to become a member of a writers' group in Los Angeles founded by Ray Bradbury and Sid Stebel. A number of her short stories were collected in *The Cry of the Tinamou* (1997), published by the University of Nebraska Press.

Her second novel, *The Lost Traveler* ([1958] 1995), set in the late 1920s in two High Plains towns, broadens the gender questions posed by a young woman into a novelized inquiry into kinship roles and family obligations. The shifting fortunes and pattern of self-deception that beset Des Tannehill, a small-town gambler, remind the reader of Eugene O'Neill's *The Iceman Cometh,* a play that dramatizes contradictory impulses, broken dreams, and squandered talent.

Loosely based on Sanora's adolescent experiences in the Oklahoma Panhandle and western Kansas, *The Lost Traveler* portrays a family whose situation as outsiders in the community exacerbates the conflicts and affections expressed within the family. The figure of the gambler, the "lost traveler," is both a character study and a sociohistorical commentary on the passing of the late frontier, a time when development, genteel values, and conservative politics succeeded an earlier order that attracted restless, independent figures like Des. The new order of respectability and moral conventions stifled people like Des, who, endowed, for better or worse, with vitality and spirit of adventure, energized early western settlement.

Prompted by her English literary agent, Patience Ross, Babb wrote a novelized memoir titled *An Owl on Every Post*, based on her family's attempt to grow broomcorn on a dryland farm in eastern Colorado shortly before World War I. Babb enchants the reader with closely detailed evocations of the mystery, wonder, and poetry of the High Plains she knew as a child. A work of delicate ecological sensitivity, *Owl* examines a tiny parcel of the immense Plains, revealing the problematic relationships of human beings constrained by isolation but possessing their rich imaginative lives—as though Rachel Carson and Charlotte Brontë had written with one pen.

Dorothy Babb never married, becoming increasingly a burden on Sanora, who supported her financially and emotionally until she died at the age of eighty-five. After the breakup of his marriage to Jennie, Walter Babb wandered from Garden City to casinos in Colorado Springs and Las Vegas, then to small-time gambling locales in New Mexico, finally dying alone in a San Diego hotel and leaving his last "stake" to his daughters. Jennie, their beloved mother, married a grocer in Garden City and moved to California, channeling her frustrated desire to write into long reminiscences in letter form that helped Sanora to reconstruct early memories.

Sanora continued to publish short stories and poems into her eighties. Shortly after she turned ninety-seven on April 21, 2004, her novel of loss, human dignity, and endurance, *Whose Names Are Unknown*, finally appeared in print, testimony to an individual's endurance and the longevity of good works. Knitting explosive labor issues into a quietly powerful narrative of a people in distress, Babb's novel is situated in the intimacy of family life, avoiding formulaic stereotypes and sentimentalizing. Her displaced farmers are people whom we might have known rather than figures in a fable of exodus (*The Grapes of Wrath*) or proletarian heroes (Arnold B. Armstrong's *Parched Earth*).[5]

The lives of people uprooted from their homes and engaged as itinerant workers—the proletariat of our time—continues to be a timely, if neglected, subject. Migrant farmworkers continue to do the planting and harvesting and experience the difficulties of lives in transit that Sanora describes. Moreover, we still do not know their names.

6 EPILOGUE
Letters from the Fields

Tensions between field workers and growers erupted in impromptu strike activity spreading throughout Kern County cotton fields in the fall of 1938. Migrant workers, many of whom were unfamiliar with or hostile to unions, participated in the cotton strikes. Understaffed labor organizers attempted to channel the anger and frustration of the workers into unified action. It appeared for a time that some great awakening, long hoped for, was finally underway. The D.F. groups in the government camps, Tom Collins wrote Sanora, had paved the way for the informal workers' councils and collective initiatives that the UCAPAWA hoped to consolidate into a broad-based labor front—something that in fact never materialized. Returning to Los Angeles in late October 1938, Sanora received letters from people in the camps, including two from workers whom she had met shortly before she left the fields and who had become active with the C.I.O. In the letters the organizers report on the workers' growing political awareness, expressing appreciation for Sanora's role in helping the dispossessed get back on their feet and assert their rights. Better than anyone Tom Collins knew what her role had been and what remained for her to do.

Buttonwillow, California

November 5, 1938
Miss Sanora Babb,
Dear friend, will answer your letter received Monday evening, thanking you for the cigarettes that you sent us which all three of us appreciated and enjoyed so much and we taken one pack a piece and gave some to the other brothers who fought so hard to make the strike a success and to organize this community in which we live to try and better labor conditions around Buttonwillow. The strike was announced over at Shafter

Thursday night. We didnt get the dollar that we asked for, but I am proud to say that we didnt loose all together either, for we did get more than 75 cents per hundred pounds. Some of them are paying from 85 cents to one dollar per hundred pounds so you can see that we didnt loose completely for which we fought so hard to gain. There was so many that lost self confidence because we didn't win in 2 or three weeks and went back to the end. I really think that we gained an awful lot dont you Miss Babb if nothing else but experience and will get together and work harder to organize in a way that we will stick together like brothers and sisters should in a union that is as good as the one which we belong to, the CIO who fought so hard to better labor conditions. Here in this part of the Valley like Brother Myers and Sister McCormick and Dorothy Ray and brothers and sisters from Hollywood and brothers from other parts of the country we all appreciated having you with us for we had such a nice time and the others too. I have forgotten their names but I havent forgot the courtesy that all of you showed us and tell them hello for us and if it is ever so that you and others can come up again I will be more than glad to show you around some of the other camps that we didnt get to see and to show you what the people have to put up with in the rainy season. Tomorrow I am going to take some snapshots of some of the other camps that we didn't get to visit and will send you some of them if you would like to have some of them so you can show your friends how a cotton picker has to live to get to work for John Farmer in this part of California. A guy just as well stay in one camp as the other if he lives in any of them for he wouldnt better his condition any to move in any other camp for they are all about the same. I havent seen Dixon [Riley] in a few days. I moved him over to the Government camp at Shafter and Burnham moved north some where, well I guess I had better sign off for the present. I guess you will be getting tired of reading by this time you get this read. Hoping to hear from you again Miss Babb soon. I will send the sizes that Mrs. Blankenship wrote on a slip of paper and if you will forgive me for waiting so long to answer I wanted to see how the strike came out so I could tell you I guess you have already found out by now. Next time it wont be so long.

Sincerely

Henry V. Selb

Arvin, California

November 9, 1939
Dear Friend,

Guess I will give you a little surprise since I have your address. Mr. and Mrs. Rogers were up last night and today & I showed them around part of this districk, which is known as part of the Arvin districk.

I moved from Buttonwillow just after the strike last fall, have spent most of the time in Kern County since I came to California, have been in Arvin since Sept. 1st. We are in another strike now & have been out 38 days today.

I sure would be glad to see you and sis /Dorothy Babb/ and would be glade to have you come to Arvin and look around, you might see something that would help you in your work.

I sure was glade to meet Mr. Rogers again, we have several of the Hollywood boys & girls up with us and they have been a good help to us. We had a moving picture show here tonight. I think we will have one once a week through the next year.

We are having a pie supper with an intertainment to raise funds. This is one strike we have started out to win and we are going to win if we have to strike for the next twelve months, we must win and break the Associated Farmers down.

I have walked the picket line untill—& walk it in my sleep. There are many things I would like to write but will save them for some other time. Good by and good luck.

A union friend

Riley Dixon

Tom Collins to Sanora, 1938–9:

I shall try to make a complete report to which you are entitled, inasmuch as you are deeply involved in the changes taking place, because you are one of us and have done so much to bring us courage and a peep at the dawn of a better day for the farmers.

....

. . . you have a dignified, quiet and persuasive method for imparting instruction and knowledge to people who are far from being schooled in the three r's. Of course, I am most thankful for what you have done for our boys, and they in turn are also thankful. If it were at all possible, the CIO or others should use your same simple system, but there is only one YOU.

....

Frankly, I feel that you can do your best work for the agricultural and industrial workers by and through the power of the written word. You have the unusual ability possessed by a few writers to do a POWERFUL bit of work. The field is rapidly being filled with organizers. Whatever you write will be of great assistance to the workers and organizers. . . .

NOTES

Notes to Preface

1. In the following I use the *Webster's New Collegiate Dictionary* (1976) definition of "refugee," "one that flees for safety," a condition initially describing the dusted-out farmers who subsequently found work as migrants, defined by *Webster's* as "person[s] who mov[e] regularly in order to find work esp. in harvesting crops." Also see Collins, who wrote in 1941, "As with those refugees from the Infertile Crescent, few of these Dust Bowlers succeed in a satisfactory early resettlement, and many have to keep on for years as seasonal, constant migrants" (*America's Own Refugees*, 10–11).

2. *Austin American-Statesman*, 14 December 2003. Until recently Ascencio was a visiting researcher at the Center for U.S.-Mexican Studies at the University of California, San Diego.

3. Jeffrey Passel, "Mexican Immigration to the U.S.: The Latest Estimates," *Migration Information Source* (August 2005).

4. Cited by Dean E. Murphy, "Imagining Life without Illegal Immigrants," *New York Times*, 11 January 2004.

5. For two recent Mexican migrant narratives, see Gonzalez, *Crossing Vines* (2003); and Martinez, *Crossing Over* (2001).

6. Sanora Babb gave approximately 250 transparencies and a total of 43 prints and negatives to the Harry Ransom Humanities Research Center at the University of Texas, from which the selection represented here derives. A number of the prints in the selection were made from transparencies because the original negatives were lost or destroyed. The possibility exists, of course, that transparent film was used to make the transparencies, in which case there would be no negatives. Babb attributed the transparencies to Dorothy Babb and the remaining photos to Dorothy and herself. A Leica (35 mm) and a Rolleicord (2$^{1}/_{2}$") were used to make the photos. Note that the photo on page 58 (picket captain) is a composite; i.e., one image is superimposed on another. The photograph titles are Sanora's own or are adapted from them.

Introduction

1. Eitner 67.

2. Billington 90–92.

3. I use Webb's description of the Great Plains environment. See Webb, chap. 1.

4. Webb, 3.

5. On the special conditions of the High Plains grasslands, see Worster, *Under Western Skies*, chap. 7. For an explanation of dry farming, see Hargreaves.

6. Among Sanora Babb's papers is a birth certificate from the Leavenworth (Kan-

sas) Hospital. I found no record of it, however, in the city or county clerk's office there. Sanora explained to me that a physician in Leavenworth, a friend of her maternal grandparents, signed the certificate in order to satisfy their wish that Sanora be listed as born in Kansas, not in Oklahoma Territory. The territories, in the grandmother's view, were not a proper birthplace.

7. Gregory calls the "refugee notion" misleading; it "elevates the tragic connotations of the migration," he writes (10). Yet, as Sanora Babb remarked to me, "refugee" is more accurate than "migrant," which suggests seasonal labor as a permanent occupation.

8. The Nash and Rogers photographs are located in the photographic collection of the Harry Ransom Humanities Research Center, University of Texas.

9. Eudora Welty, who worked in Mississippi for the Farm Security Administration, made no apologies for the "crudities" of her photographs. "A better and less ignorant photographer," she wrote, "would certainly have come up with better pictures, but not these pictures; for he could hardly have been as well positioned as I was, moving through the scene openly and yet invisibly because I was part of it, born into it, taken for granted" (n.p.).

10. Wright, *White Man Listen!* 145.

11. On cultural memory, see Nora's three-volume *Realms of Memory*.

12. My main sources are Sassen; Bottomly; Piore; Wilson; Islas; A. B. Simmons.

Chapter 1

1. Murphy, "Imagining Life" 1, 16.

2. Briggs, Fogel, and Schmidt.

3. Cockcroft 40.

4. *New York Times* (31 May 1998): 1.

5. "Studying a Town," 1.

6. Most black migrants worked in Arizona's cotton fields. See LeSeur.

7. The Dust Bowl balladeer Woody Guthrie wrote, "Almost everybody is a Okie now days. That means you ain't got no home, or don't know how long you're gonna have the one you are in. Sort of means, too, that you're out of a job. Or owe more than you can rake and scrape" (Lomax 213). Although "Dust Bowl" and "Okies" inaccurately describe the origins of most of the refugees, I use these terms for the sake of convenience.

8. Weisiger 10.

9. The impoverished condition of Dust Bowl people, who were willing to work for lower wages than Mexican workers, attracted public attention for several reasons. The first had to do with race: apart from being American citizens, the majority of the uprooted were white. Moreover, with increasing numbers, their need for schools, medical care, and relief posed unusual demands on county treasuries. Despite reluctance on the part of many displaced farmers to participate in unions, with the arrival of native-born Anglo workers, as Guerin-Gonzales points out, union organizers succeeded in obtaining concessions from owners through widely publicized strikes (124). Finally, the human drama of the uprooted Okies attracted journalists, social scientists, novelists, and FSA photographers, who were effective in polarizing political debate, stirring public sympathy for the displaced, and prompting temporary relief.

10. *Factories in the Fields* 199.

11. Some two-thirds of the total resident population chose not to leave their Dust Bowl homes. They were people, writes Timothy Egan, "who stayed behind, for lack of money or lack of sense, . . . people who hunkered down out of loyalty or stubbornness, who believed in tomorrow because it was all they had in the bank" (9–10).

12. Loftis 9.

13. Loftis 19.

14. The English historian T. H. Watkins writes, "The New Dealers had been no more successful in fitting these contrary Anglo-Saxon farmers into the mold of sedate and

obedient citizen-laborers than the CP/USA had been in persuading them to join the rest of the proletariat to pull down capitalism and stamp it into ruins. This new wave of migrants, like most Americans, entertained dreams of becoming part of the capitalist system—or at least part of the comfortable middle class—and they were not particularly interested in spending the rest of their lives working some corporate farm" (458).

15. *Factories in the Fields* chap. 14; Stein 97–103; Gregory 88–100.

16. Watkins 441.

17. Watkins 443.

18. Initially (ca. 1934) the arrival of Dust Bowl refugees caused little alarm or resentment among Californians. Not even their numbers, estimated as high as 600,000, risked creating what James N. Gregory terms "migration anxiety" (79) if earlier patterns of settlement had been followed. Among the causes of growing resentment and political rankling among Californians was the fact that the Anglo refugee workers were drawn to agricultural counties rather than spreading throughout the state. Unlike earlier farmworkers—mainly ethnic minorities—the Dust Bowl people came to stay, placing severe strains on county governments and local residents. Protectionist attitudes were ingrained among many Californians (Gregory 79). Chinese, Japanese, Filipino, and Mexican farmworkers had each in turn experienced hostility and ultimately exclusion. Many communities, moreover, had strict vagrancy laws. It was thought that transient workers ("tramps") might fuel radical activity such as the Industrial Workers of the World (IWW) had sponsored. In the small rural communities the Okies were often viewed as a degraded, immoral people used to living in squalor and dependent on the dole. Finally, growing tensions between farm laborers and growers became highly contested issues affecting political legislation and requiring legal judication. See Stein 44–64.

19. See Taylor and Rowell, "Refugee Labor" 246.

20. Letter, Paul S. Taylor to Dr. Lowry Nelson, Emergency Relief Administration, State of California, 17 April 1935, Taylor Papers, Bancroft Library, University of California, Berkeley.

21. Bias against the Dust Bowl refugees had less to do with race or ethnicity than with their impoverished, transient condition and status as outsiders. See Gregory 79.

22. Baldwin chap. 6.

23. In *Whose Names Are Unknown* the black field worker Garrison is instrumental in convincing the field workers to demonstrate for better wages and conditions. Note that Dorothy Babb's photographs include black and Mexican field workers. "In the Imperial Valley group of transients there were only eight Negro families from Oklahoma and three Mexican families from Texas and Arizona. Some day the racial aspects of this migration to the West may assume greater importance" (Taylor and Rowell, "Refugee Labor" 250).

24. See Taylor and Rowell, "Refugee Labor" 245.

25. Baldwin 268–269.

26. Baldwin chap. 9.

27. Interviews with Julia King Marken (17 October 2002; 19 April 2004); Charlie King (16 October 2002; 19 April 2005); Harlan King (9 September 2002); 21 November 2003). On the King family as musicians, see Fanslow.

28. Interview with Dorothy Healey (5 June 2002).

29. See DeMott xxviii. Also, Benson, *Looking* 83–85.

30. *True Adventures* 296.

31. *Whose Names Are Unknown* appeared in a University of Oklahoma Press edition in 2004. Credit for encouraging Babb to release her manuscript for publication belongs mainly to her agent, Joanne Dearcopp. Lawrence Rodgers provides a very useful introduction.

32. See Simmons, *Introduction to Russian Realism* 5.

33. This is not altogether correct. Under Stryker's tutelage FSA photographers such as Marion Post Wolcott included as subjects urban areas and people privileged by their wealth.

34. In 1938 the photographer Horace Bristol accompanied Steinbeck into the fields for a *Life* assignment. Their collaboration never appeared in print.

35. Hurley 56–60.

36. "Putting America on Record" 96.

37. Hurley 90.

38. Meltzer 184.

39. Levine 17.

40. Not all critics share this view. Yet it is true that promotion of the FSA's programs was at the heart of Stryker's photography project. A balanced view of the FSA photographers' work must therefore include all photos, not simply those that were used to publicize the refugees' plight and prompt federal funding.

41. My principal sources for the following discussion are Berger and Mohr; Batchen; Curtis; Hurley; Lange and Taylor; Meltzer; Partridge; Salgado; Shloss; Sontag; Stott; Stryker and Wood.

42. Tucker et al.

43. Ganzel 10.

Chapter 2

1. *Factories* 199.

2. McWilliams, *Factories* 212.

3. McWilliams, *Factories* 212.

4. McWilliams, *Factories* 228.

5. Gregory 62.

6. Gregory 95.

7. McWilliams, *Factories* 268.

8. See Arax and Wartzman for an example of Okies who became wealthy growers.

Chapter 3

1. See Benson; DeMott; T. Collins.

Chapter 4

1. Carter explains: "Westward with declining precipitation, the degree of leaching drops. Near the 100th meridian, the boundary is met where the amount of precipitation is no longer able to move through the ground to maintain a permanent water table, which means that the ground is annually wet to some depth and thereafter dries out" (351).

2. From a gender perspective, Babb's approach to her subject is identifiably relational. On gender and difference, see Gilligan; Johnson.

3. This deserves further study. On ecofeminist questions, my sources are Murphy; Warren; Mellor.

Chapter 5

1. Gill.

2. Boxall.

3. Arax and Wartzman.

4. See Donahue.

5. Edmund Wilson wrote about Steinbeck's novel that "these Okies . . . do not exist for him [Steinbeck] quite seriously as people."

BIBLIOGRAPHY

Books and Periodicals

Agee, James, and Walker Evans. *Let Us Now Praise Famous Men: Three Tenant Families.* Boston: Houghton Mifflin, 1939.

Arax, Mark. "A Lost Tribe's Journey to a Land of Broken Promises." *Los Angeles Times* (25 August 2002): A1, A25–26.

Arax, Mark, and Rick Wartzman. *The King of California: J. G. Boswell and the Making of a Secret American Empire.* New York: Public Affairs, 2003.

Armstrong, Arnold B. *Parched Earth.* New York: Macmillan, 1934.

Babb, Sanora. *The Dark Earth & Other Stories from the Great Depression.* Santa Barbara, CA: Capra Press, 1987.

———. *An Owl on Every Post.* Albuquerque: University of New Mexico Press, 1994.

———. *The Lost Traveler.* Introd. Douglas Wixson. Albuquerque: University of New Mexico Press, 1995.

———. *The Cry of the Tinamou.* Introd. Alan Wald. Lincoln: University of Nebraska Press, 1997.

———. *Whose Names Are Unknown.* Introd. Lawrence R. Rodgers. Norman: University of Oklahoma Press, 2004.

Baldwin, Sidney. *Poverty and Politics: The Rise and Decline of the Farm Security Administration.* Chapel Hill: University of North Carolina Press, 1968.

Barrio, Raymond. *The Plum Pickers.* New York: Harper & Row, 1969.

Batchen, Geoffrey. *Each Wild Idea: Writing, Photography, History.* Cambridge, MA: MIT Press, 2001.

———. "'To Tom, Who Lived It': John Steinbeck and the Man from Weedpatch." *Journal of Modern Literature* 5 (April 1976): 151–194.

Benson, Jackson J. *Looking for Steinbeck's Ghost.* Norman: University of Oklahoma Press, 1988.

———. *The True Adventures of John Steinbeck.* New York: Viking Press, 1988.

Berger, John. *Another Way of Seeing.* Harmondsworth: Penguin, 1972.

Berger, John, and Jean Mohr. *Another Way of Telling.* New York: Pantheon, 1982.

Berger, Peter L., with Brigitte Berger and Hansfried Kellner. *The Homeless Mind: Modernization and Consciousness.* New York: Random House, 1973.

Billington, Ray. *Land of Savagery, Land of Promise.* New York: Norton, 1981.

Blew, Mary Clearman. *Bone Deep in Landscape.* Norman: University of Oklahoma Press, 1999.

Blouet, Brian W. *The Great Plains: Environment and Culture.* Lincoln: University of Nebraska Press, 1979.

Blouet, Brian W., and Frederick C. Luebke, eds. *The Great Plains: Environment and Culture.* Lincoln: University of Nebraska Press, 1979.

Bonnifield, Paul. *The Dust Bowl: Men, Dirt and Depression.* Albuquerque: University of New Mexico Press, 1979.

Bottomly, Gillian. *From Another Place: Migration and the Politics of Culture.* London: Cambridge University Press, 1992.

Boxall, Bettina. "Migrants' New Roots Transform Rural Life." *Los Angeles Times* (20 April 1999): A1, A22.

Briggs, Vernon M., Jr., Walter Fogel, and Fred H. Schmidt. *The Chicano Worker.* Austin: University of Texas Press, 1977.

Brown, Patricia Leigh. "Oklahomans Try to Save Their California Culture." *New York Times* (5 February 2002): A22.

Burgin, Victor. *In/Different Spaces: Place and Memory in Visual Culture.* Berkeley: University of California Press, 1996.

Burns, Nancy. *The Collapse of Small Towns on the Great Plains.* Emporia, KS: Emporia State University, 1982.

Caldwell, Erskine, and Margaret Bourke-White. *Say, Is This the U.S.A.* New York: Da Capo Press, 1977.

Callahan, Sean, ed. *The Photographs of Margaret Bourke-White.* Boston: New York Graphic Society, 1975.

Camus, Albert. "L'Homme révolte." In *Essais,* ed. R. Quillot and L. Faucon. Paris: Bibliothèque de la Pléiade, 1965.

Carlebach, Michael L. "Documentary and Propaganda: The Photographs of the Farm Security Administration." *Journal of Decorative and Propaganda Arts* 8 (spring 1988): 6–25.

Chase, Stuart. *Rich Land, Poor Land.* New York: McGraw-Hill, 1936.

Cockcroft, James D. *Outlaws in the Promised Land: Mexican Immigrant Workers and America's Future.* New York: Grove Press, 1986.

Collins, Henry Hill, Jr. *America's Own Refugees.* Princeton, NJ: Princeton University Press, 1941.

Collins, Thomas. *Reports from Arvin Migratory Labor Camp* (1936). Unedited MSS with FSA papers. Kern County Library System, Bakersfield, CA.

———. "Field Reports" (unedited). FSA Archives, NARA-Pacific Region, San Bruno, CA.

Comer, Krista. *Landscapes of the New West: Gender and Geography in Contemporary Women's Writing.* Chapel Hill: University of North Carolina Press, 1999.

Cook, Sylvia J. *From Tobacco Road to Route 66: The Southern Poor White in Fiction.* Chapel Hill: University of North Carolina Press, 1976.

Cox, Martha Beasley. "Fact into Fiction in *The Grapes of Wrath*: The Weedpatch and Arvin Camps." In *John Steinbeck: East and West,* ed. Tetsumaro Hayashi, Yasuo Hashiguchi, and Richard F. Peterson. Muncie, IN: Steinbeck Monograph Series No. 8 (1978): 12–21.

Curtis, James. *Mind's Eye, Mind's Truth: FSA Photography Reconsidered.* Philadelphia: Temple University Press, 1989.

Daniel, Cletus E. *Bitter Harvest: A History of California Farm Workers, 1870–1941.* Berkeley: University of California Press, 1981.

DeMott, Robert J., ed. *Working Days: The Journals of "The Grapes of Wrath," 1938–1941.* New York: Viking Press, 1989.

Donahue, Debra L. *The Western Range Revisted: Removing Livestock from Public Lands to Conserve Native Biodiversity.* Norman: University of Oklahoma Press, 1999.

"The Dust Bowl Journal: A Collection of Pictures and Stories." Supplement. *Arvin Tiller/Lamont Reporter* (2 October 1996).

Egan, Timothy. *The Worst Hard Time.* New York: Houghton Mifflin, 2006.

Eitner, Walter. *Walt Whitman's Western Jaunt.* Lawrence: Regents Press of Kansas, 1981.

Fanslow, Robin. "Voices from the Dust Bowl: The Charles L. Todd and Robert Sonkin Collection." *Folklife Center News* 20 (spring 1998): 3–9.

Fetterley, Judith, and Marjorie Pryse. *Writing out of Place: Regionalism, Women, and American Literary Culture.* Urbana: University of Illinois Press, 2003.

Fleischhauer, Carl, and Beverly W. Brannan, eds. *Documenting America, 1935–1943*. Berkeley: University of California Press, 1988.

Flores, Dan. *The Natural West: Environmental History in the Great Plains and Rocky Mountains*. Norman: University of Oklahoma Press, 2001.

Ganzel, Bill. *Dust Bowl Descent*. Lincoln: University of Nebraska Press, 1984.

Garcia, Dawn. "Memories of Dust Bowl Migrants Conjure up Bias of Past." *San Francisco Chronicle* (20 September 1991): A1.

Gill, Richardson B. *The Great Maya Droughts*. Albuquerque: University of New Mexico Press, 2001.

Gilligan, Carol. *In a Different Voice: Psychological Theory and Women's Development*. Cambridge, MA: Harvard University Press, 1982.

Goldfarb, Ronald L. *A Caste of Despair: Migrant Farm Workers*. Ames: Iowa State University Press, 1981.

González, Rigoberto. *Crossing Vines: A Novel*. Norman: University of Oklahoma Press, 2001.

"The Grapes of Wrath, Again." *The Economist* (10 September 2005): 36.

Gregg, Josiah. *Commerce of the Prairies* (1844). Ed. Max L. Moorhead. Norman: University of Oklahoma Press, 1954.

Gregory, James N. *American Exodus: The Dust Bowl Migration and Okie Culture in California*. New York: Oxford University Press, 1989.

Griffith, David, and Ed Kissam. *Working Poor: Farmworkers in the United States*. Philadelphia: Temple University Press, 1995.

Guerin-Gonzales, Camille. *Mexican Workers and American Dreams: Immigration, Repatriation, and California Farm Labor, 1900–1939*. New Brunswick, NJ: Rutgers University Press, 1994.

Gutman, Judith Mara. *Lewis W. Hine and the American Conscience*. New York: Walker, 1968.

Halbwachs, Maurice. *On Collective Memory*. Ed. and trans. Lewis L. Coser. Chicago: University of Chicago Press, 1992.

Handbook of Labor Statistics. Ed. Eva E. Jacobs. Lanham, MD: Bernan Press, 2001.

Hargreaves, Mary W. M. *Dry Farming in the Northern Great Plains*. Cambridge, MA: Harvard University Press, 1957.

Haslam, Gerald W. *Okies: Selected Stories*. Santa Barbara, CA: Peregrine Smith, 1975.

Healey, Dorothy, and Maurice Isserman. *California Red: A Life in the American Communist Party*. Urbana: University of Illinois Press, 1993.

Henderson, Caroline. *Letters from the Dust Bowl*. Ed. Alvin O. Turner. Norman: University of Oklahoma Press, 2001.

———. *The Suitcase Farming Frontier: A Study in the Historical Geography of the Central Great Plains*. Lincoln: University of Nebraska Press, 1973.

Hewes, Leslie. "Agricultural Risk in the Great Plains." In Blouet and Luebke 157–185.

Hine, Robert V. *The American West, an Interpretative History*. Boston: Little, Brown, 1973.

Hintz, Joy. *Poverty, Prejudice, Power, Politics: Migrants Speak about Their Lives*. Columbus, OH: Avonelle Associates, 1981.

Hurley, F. Jack. *Roy Stryker and the Development of Documentary Photography in the Thirties*. Baton Rouge: Louisiana State University Press, 1974.

Hurt, R. Douglas. *The Dust Bowl: An Agricultural and Social History*. Chicago: Nelson-Hall, 1984.

Igler, David. *Industrial Cowboys: Miller and Lux and the Transformation of the Far West, 1850–1920*. Berkeley: University of California, 2001.

Islas, Arturo. *On the Bridge, at the Border: Migrants and Immigrants*. Stanford: Stanford Center for Chicano Research, 1990.

Jimenez, Francisco. *The Circuit: Stories from the Life of a Migrant Child*. Albuquerque: University of New Mexico Press, 1997.

Johnson, Barbara. *A World of Difference*. Baltimore: Johns Hopkins University Press, 1987.

Johnson, Stephen, ed. Text by Gerald Haslam. *The Great Central Valley: California's Heartland*. Berkeley: University of California Press, 1993.

Kaplan, Robert D. *An Empire Wilderness*. New York: Random House, 1998.

Kelton, Elmer. *The Time It Never Rained*. Fort Worth: Texas Christian University Press, 1984.

Kilborn, Peter T. "Bucking Trend, They Stay, Held by Family and Friends." *New York Times* (2 December 2003): A1, A28.

Kuberski, Philip. *The Persistence of Memory: Organism, Myth, Text*. Berkeley: University of California Press, 1992.

Kraenzel, Carl Frederick. *The Great Plains in Transition*. Norman: University of Oklahoma Press, 1955.

Lange, Dorothea, and Paul Schuster Taylor. *An American Exodus: A Record of Human Erosion*. New York: Reynal and Hitchcock, 1939.

LeSeur, Geta J. *Not All Okies Are White*. Columbia: University of Missouri Press, 2000.

Levine, Lawrence W. "Photography and the History of the American People in the 1930s and 1940s." In Fleischhauer and Brannan 15–42.

Lewis, M. H., ed. *Migratory Labor in California*. San Francisco: State Relief Administration of California, 1939.

Light, Ken. *Witness in Our Time: Working Lives of Documentary Photographers*. Washington, DC: Smithsonian Institution Press, 2000.

Limerick, Patricia Nelson. *The Legacy of Conquest: The Unbroken Past of the American West*. New York: Norton, 1987.

Loftis, Anne. *Witnesses to the Struggle: Imaging the 1930s California Labor Movement*. Reno: University of Nevada Press, 1998.

Loh, Jules. "Transplanted Okies Left Their Mark on California." *Hutchinson (Kansas) News* (6 September 1992): 30.

Lomax, Alan, comp. *Hard-Hitting Songs for Hard-Hit People*. New York: Oak Publications, 1967.

Longo, Peter J., and David W. Yoskowitz, eds. *Water on the Great Plains: Issues and Policies*. Lubbock: Texas Tech University Press, 2002.

Lord, Russell. *To Hold This Soil*. Washington, DC: U.S. Department of Agriculture, 1938.

MacPhee, Graham. *The Architecture of the Visible*. London: Continuum, 2002.

Majka, Linda C., and Theo J. Majka. *Farm Workers, Agribusiness, and the State*. Philadelphia: Temple University Press, 1982.

Martinez, Ruben. *Crossing Over: A Mexican Family on the Migrant Trail*. New York: Picador, 2001.

Marshall, James M. *Land Fever: Dispossession and the Frontier Myth*. Lexington: University Press of Kentucky, 1976.

McNeill, William, and Ruth S. Adams, eds. *Human Migration: Patterns and Policies*. Bloomington: Indiana University Press, 1978.

McWilliams, Carey. *Southern California Country, an Island in the Land*. New York: Duell, Sloan and Pearce, 1946.

———. *Factories in the Fields: The Story of Migratory Farm Labor in California*. Foreword by Douglas C. Sackman. Berkeley: University of California Press, 1999.

Mellor, Mary. *Feminism and Ecology*. Cambridge: Polity Press, 1997.

Meltzer, Milton. *Dorothea Lange, a Photographer's Life*. New York: Farrar, Straus and Giroux, 1978.

Merleau-Ponty, Maurice. *The Phenomenology of Perception*. Trans. Colin Smith. Boston: Routledge and Kegan Paul, 1962.

Migrant Farm Labor: The Problem and How to Meet It. Washington, DC: FSA, Department of Agriculture, 1940.

Morgan, Dan. *Rising in the West.* New York: Alfred A. Knopf, 1992.

Murphy, Dean E. "Southern California Water Officials Race Deadline Tonight," *New York Times* (31 December 2002): A14.

———. "Imagining Life without Illegal Immigrants." *New York Times* (11 January 2004): 1, 16.

Murphy, Patrick D. *Literature, Nature and Others: Ecofeminist Critique.* Albany: State University of New York Press, 1995.

Nelson, Cary. *Repression and Recovery: Modern American Poetry and the Politics of Cultural Memory, 1910–1945.* Madison: University of Wisconsin Press, 1989.

———. *Revolutionary Memory: Recovering the Poetry of the American Left.* New York: Routledge, 2001.

Nora, Pierre, ed. *Realms of Memory.* 3 vols. Trans. Lawrence D. Kritzman. New York: Columbia University Press, 1996.

North, Michael. *Camera Works: Photography and the Twentieth- Century Word.* New York: Oxford University Press, 2005.

Nugent, Walter. *Into the West: The Story of Its People.* New York: Vintage, 2003.

Parini, Jay. *John Steinbeck: A Biography.* London: Heinemann, 1994.

Partridge, Elizabeth, ed. *Dorothea Lange, a Visual Life.* Washington, DC: Smithsonian Institution Press, 1994.

Pawel, Miriam. "Farmworkers Reap Little as Union Strays from Its Roots." Los Angeles Times (8 January 2006): A1, A24–26.

Pincetl, Stephanie S. *Transforming California: A Political History of Land Use and Development.* Baltimore: Johns Hopkins University Press, 1999.

Piore, Michael J. *Birds of Passage: Migrant Labor and Industrial Societies.* London: Cambridge University Press, 1979.

Powell, John Wesley. *Report on the Lands of the Arid Regions.* Washington, DC, 1878.

Prescott, Jerome, ed. *American at the Crossroads: Great Photographs from the Thirties.* New York: Smithmark, 1995.

"Putting America on Record." *Saturday Review of Literature* (17 December 1938): 96.

Raban, Jonathan. *Bad Land: An American Romance.* New York: Pantheon, 1996.

Reisner, Marc. *Cadillac Desert: The American West and Its Disappearing Water.* New York: Viking Press, 1986.

Richards, Bill. "Many Rural Regions Are Growing Again; A Reason: Technology." *Wall Street Journal* (22 November 1994): A1, A5.

Rosenblum, Naomi. *A History of Women Photographers.* New York: Abbeville Press, 1994.

Rosowski, Susan J. *The Voyage Perilous: Willa Cather's Romanticism.* Lincoln: University of Nebraska Press, 1986.

Rothstein, Arthur. *Documentary Photography.* Boston: Focal Press, 1986.

Salgado, Sebastião. *Humanity in Transition.* Paris: Amazonas Image, 2000.

Sassen, Saskia. *Guests and Aliens.* New York: New Press, 1999.

Schlissel, Lillian. "The Frontier Family: Dislocation and the American Experience." In *Making America: The Society and Culture of the United States,* ed. Luther S. Luedtke. Chapel Hill: University of North Carolina Press, 1992.

Schlosser, Eric. "In the Strawberry Fields." *Atlantic Monthly* (November 1995): 80–108.

Shannon, Fred A. *The Farmer's Last Frontier.* New York: Holt, Rinehart and Winston, 1966.

Shindo, Charles J. *Dust Bowl Migrants in the American Imagination.* Lawrence: University Press of Kansas, 1997.

Shloss, Carol. *In Visible Light: Photography and the American Writer, 1840–1940.* New York: Oxford University Press, 1987.

Simmons, Alan B., ed. *International Migration: Refugee Flows and Human Rights in North America: The Impact of Free Trade and Restructuring.* New York: Center for Migration Studies, 1996.

Simmons, Ernest J. *Introduction to Russian Realism.* Bloomington: Indiana University Press, 1965.

Simson, Grace Heilman. *The Rise of the Labor Movement in Los Angeles*. Berkeley: University of California Press, 1955.

Sontag, Susan. *On Photography*. New York: Farrar, Straus and Giroux, 1977.

———. *Regarding the Pain of Suffering*. New York: Farrar, Straus and Giroux, 2003.

Starr, Kevin. *Endangered Dreams: The Great Depression in California*. New York: Oxford University Press, 1996.

Stauffer, Helen Winter. *Mari Sandoz, Story Catcher of the Plains*. Lincoln: University of Nebraska Press, 1982.

Stegner, Wallace. *Beyond the Hundredth Meridian: John Wesley Powell and the Second Opening of the West*. New York: Penguin, 1982.

Stein, Walter J. *California and the Dust Bowl Migration*. Westport, CT: Greenwood Press, 1973.

Steinbeck, John. *The Grapes of Wrath*. New York: Viking Press, 1939.

———. *The Harvest Gypsies*. Introd. Charles Wollenberg. Berkeley: Heyday Books, 1988.

Street, Richard Steven. *Photographing Farmworkers in California*. Stanford, CA: Stanford University Press, 2004.

"Studying a Town to Death." *Rachel's Environment & Health Weekly* 643 (25 March 1999): 1–2.

Stott, William. *Documentary Expression and Thirties America*. New York: Oxford University Press, 1973.

Stout, Janis P. *Willa Cather: The Writer and Her World*. Charlottesville: University Press of Virginia, 2000.

Stryker, Roy Emerson, and Nancy Wood. *In This Proud Land: America 1935–1943 as Seen in the FSA Photographs*. Greenwich, CT: New York Graphic Society, 1973.

Taylor, Paul. "Synopsis of Survey of Migratory Labor Problems in California." Resettlement Administration, San Francisco, 1938.

Taylor, Paul, and Edward J. Rowell. *Refugee Labor Migration to California, 1937*. Washington, DC: U.S. Department of Labor, 1937.

———. *Patterns of Agricultural Labor Migration within California*, Washington, DC: U.S. Department of Labor, Serial No. R. 840 (1938).

———. "Refugee Labor Migration to California, 1937," *Monthly Labor Review* (August 1938): 240–250.

Thacker, Robert. *The Great Prairie Fact and Literary Imagination*. Albuquerque: University of New Mexico Press, 1989.

Thelen, David. *Paths of Resistance: Tradition and Dignity in Industrializing Missouri*. New York: Oxford University Press, 1986.

Todd, Charles L. "Trampling out the Vintage." *Common Sense* 8 (July 1939): 7–8, 30.

Tucker, Ann Wilkes, et al. *This Was the Photo League*. Chicago: Stephen Daiter Gallery, 2001.

Urgo, Joseph R. *Willa Cather and the Myth of American Migration*. Urbana: University of Illinois Press, 1995.

Van Hear, Nicholas. *New Diasporas: Mass Exodus, Dispersal and Regrouping of Migrant Communities*. Seattle: University of Washington Press, 1998.

Vaught, David. *Cultivating California: Growers, Speciality Crops, and Labor, 1875–1920*. Berkeley: University of California Press, 2002.

Wald, Alan. *Exiles from a Future Time: The Forging of the Mid-Twentieth-Century Literary Left*. Chapel Hill: University of North Carolina Press, 2002.

Warren, Karen J. *Ecofeminism: Women's Culture, Nature*. Bloomington: Indiana University Press, 1997.

Watkins, T. H. *The Hungry Years: A Narrative History of the Great Depression in America*. New York: Henry Holt, 2000.

Webb, Walter Prescott. *The Great Plains*. New York: Grosset & Dunlap, 1931.

Weisiger, Marsha L. *Land of Plenty: Oklahomans in the Cotton Fields of Arizona, 1933–1942.* Norman: University of Oklahoma, 1995.

Welty, Eudora. *One Time, One Place: Mississippi in the Depression.* New York: Random House, 1971.

Whitehead, Fred, and Verle Muhrer, eds. *Freethought on the Western Frontier.* Buffalo, NY: Prometheus Books, 1992.

Whitman, Walt. "The Prairie States." In *Walt Whitman: Complete Poetry and Collected Prose.* New York: Library of America, 1982.

Wilson, Edmund. *Classics and Commercials.* New York: Farrar, Straus, 1940.

Wixson, Douglas. *Worker-Writer in America: Jack Conroy and the Tradition of Midwestern Literary Radicalism, 1898–1990.* Urbana: University of Illinois Press, 1994.

Worster, Donald. *Dust Bowl: The Southern Plains in the 1930s.* New York: Oxford University Press, 1979.

———. *Rivers of Empire: Water, Aridity and the Growth of the American West.* New York: Pantheon, 1985.

———. *Under Western Skies: Nature and History in the American West.* New York: Oxford University Press, 1992.

Wright, Richard. *White Man, Listen!* Garden City, NY: Doubleday, 1957.

Libraries and Collections

A. Frank Smith, Jr. Library, Southwestern University, Georgetown, Texas

Baca County Historical Museum, Springfield, Colorado

Bancroft Library, University of California, Berkeley (Frank Taylor papers; Irving W. Woods papers; George P. Clements papers; Farm Security Administration papers)

Beaver County Library, Beaver, Oklahoma

Camp Weedpatch Archives, Arvin, California

Cherokee Strip Museum, Perry, Oklahoma

Colorado Historical Society, Denver, Colorado

Federal Records Center, San Bruno, California

Finney County Museum, Garden City, Kansas

Green Library, Stanford University, Stanford, California (John Steinbeck papers; Tillie Olsen papers)

Harry Ransom Humanities Research Center, University of Texas, Austin (Sanora Babb papers)

Labor History Archive, San Francisco State University, San Francisco, California

Library of Congress, Washington, DC (Manuscript Division, Photoduplication Service)

Los Angeles Central Library, Los Angeles, California

Morton County Historical Museum, Elkhart, Kansas

National Archives, San Bruno, California (FSA field reports)

No Man's Land Historical Society, Goodwell, Oklahoma

North Central Oklahoma Historical Association, Ponca City

Oklahoma State Historical Archives, Oklahoma City

Plains Conservation Center, Aurora, Colorado

Southern California Library for Social Studies and Research, Los Angeles

Special Collections, Charles E. Young Research Library, University of California, Los Angeles (Carey McWilliams papers)

University Library, California State University–Long Beach

Waynoka Historical Society, Waynoka, Oklahoma

On the Dirty Plate Trail

Alexander, Dorothy
Babb, Sanora
Beaumont, Imogene
Beresford, Mollie Lee Bowles
Bradbury, Ray
Campbell, Virginia
Dawson, Kathleen
Day, Faye Harrington
Frazier, John
Gordon, Bernard
Hall, Ralph, and Joanne Hall
Harrington, Irene Hutchens
Healey, Dorothy
Hethmon, Robert
Hodges, Pauline
Kendall, Gaynor
King, Charles
King, Harlan
Lee, Don
Leonard, Dwight
Lochner, Iris
Loomis, Evarts
Marken, Julie King
McAlester, Cheley Lansden
McDaniel, Wilma Elizabeth
McGrath, Alice
Michaan, John
Montgomery, Olga
Moore, Elmer
Newman, Roxana Ma
Nutter, Dell
Olsen, Sandie
Olsen, Tillie
Osteen, Ike
Parker, Allene
Parks, Nelson
Patterson, Mildred Parks
Sanford, John
Smith, Benny
Spingarn, Lawrence
Spinney, Judy
Stevenson, Janet
Switzer, Aleta
Turner, Mary
Vellas, Anastasia
Waddel, Frank
Weatherwax, Seema
Weddell, Doris
Williams, Erma (Hall)
Winfree, Inez Lansden
Wolfe, Bonnie Barrett
Young, Leigh Taylor
Zatz, Alba
Zatz, Asa

INDEX

Page numbers in italics reference photographs.

Printed in the USA
CPSIA information can be obtained
at www.ICGtesting.com
CBHW080810120424
6773CB00010B/90